Loch Lomond and The Trossachs National Park

ntice

Vol 1 – West

60 walks

Balloch, Luss, Tarbet, Arrochar, Lochgoilhead, Glenbranter, Loch Eck, Ardentinny, Benmore, Inveruglas, Inverarnan, Crianlarich and Tyndrum

Loch Lomond from Luss

Contents Vol 1 – WEST

Introduction

Balloch & Luss map 13

Tarbet & Arrochar map 37

Lochgoilhead map 67

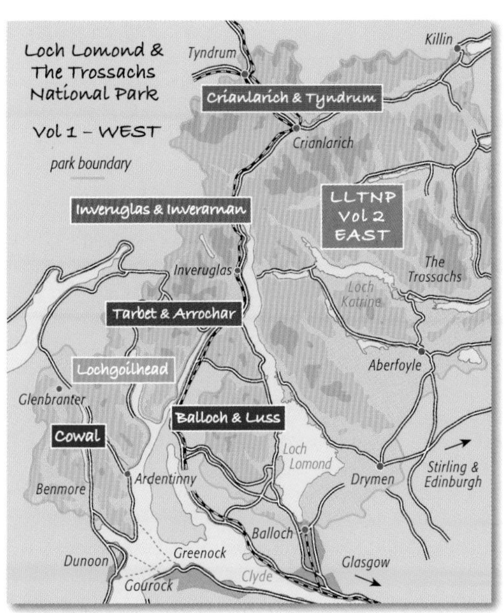

Published by Mica Publishing

ISBN 978-0-9560367-0-4

Title page: Loch Goil

Maps & design
Mica Publishing
www.micapublishing.com

Printed and bound in China
through Colorcraft Ltd.,
Hong Kong

Mica walkers' guides are
distributed by Cordee Ltd.
01455 611185
info@cordee.co.uk
www.cordee.co.uk

While every effort has been made to ensure the accuracy of this guidebook, paths and access points change over time. Sturdy footwear and waterproofs are recommended for all walks, plus a map and compass for upland walks.

Loch Lomond & The Trossachs National Park

National Park Headquarters, Balloch

From the Clyde sea-lochs warmed by the Gulf Stream, to the Highland villages of Tyndrum and Killin, much of Scotland's first National Park consists of wild land. However, the Park's location on the main west coast line of communication and its close proximity to Scotland's urban belt, means this is not a landscape devoid of people. Indeed, these factors have preserved and enriched a history and culture, lost from other parts of the Highlands by successive waves of depopulation.

The southern region of the Park includes the Highland Boundary Fault, the geological border between the fertile Lowland plains and the moors and mountains of the Highlands. An area settled, farmed and fought over by Roman and Viking invaders, Christian missionaries, kings and clans: Colquhons, MacGregors, Macfarlanes and Campbells.

The best known of these is farmer and 'outlaw' Rob Roy MacGregor. A legendary figure, but like many of his neighbours, a man with one foot in the Highlands and one in the wheeling, dealing, power and politics of the wealthy Loch Lomond and The Trossachs border lands of the 1700s. Lands through which thousands of pounds worth of cattle were herded every year, to market in the Perthshire town of Crieff.

The 18th century was a time of great change. The 1715 and 1745 Jacobite uprisings disrupted landownership and the Highland way of life. Small scale grain and cattle farming was replaced by sheep and forestry: oak for charcoal and tanning, alder for gunpowder. To the south, the growing industrial revolution drew natural resources from the area: slate, lead, iron ore and people.

At the turn of the century, with the Highlands subdued if not tamed, the first 'travellers' arrived: Thomas Pennant, Boswell and Johnstone and the Wordsworths; but it was Sir Walter Scott whose poetry and novels made The Trossachs Scotland's first tourist destination at the start of the 19th century. In Scott's wake came improved roads and railways, and with them more tourists.

Throughout the 20th century, the region came under even greater pressure as increased mobility and leisure time led to more visitors and increased demand for

- *Loch Lomond is the largest expanse of freshwater in Britain*
- *The park is 720 sq miles with a 220 mile boundary*
- *15,600 people live in the park*
- *More than 70% of Scotland's population lives less than 1 hour's travel time from the National Park*

facts from www.lochlomond-trossachs.org

golf courses, tourist developments and house building. The need for a long term plan to manage residents and visitors in harmony with the area's natural landscape and resources had finally arrived, and in 2002 the National Park came into being.

Scotland has always had a relaxed attitude to responsible walkers taking to the hills, moors and glens and since the mid-1980s the boom in recreational walking has been phenomenal. In recent years, more emphasis has been placed on encouraging recreation, especially in Scotland's extensive conifer plantations, with the creation of cycle routes and waymarked paths. Responsible access to most land and inland water became a legal right under the 2003 Land Reform Act, which also requires the National Park to identify a network of 'core paths' in the area. This path network is certain to grow in the future, offering increased opportunities for recreational walkers.

The history of this area is as much a story of its inhabitants and visitors as of its landscape, fauna and flora. For many, it is this human element which makes this National Park so special.

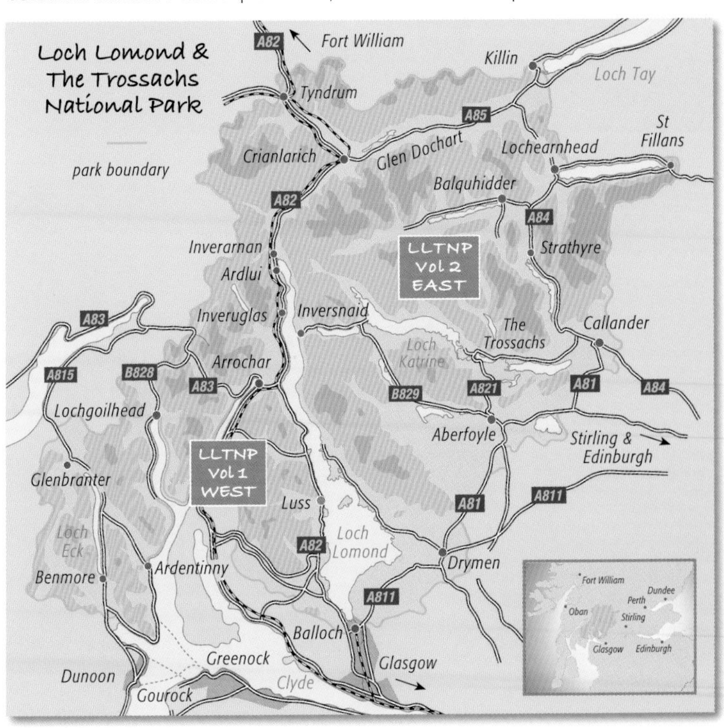

Flora & Fauna

bell heather & heather

cross-leaved heath

tormentil

blaeberry

cowberry

cloudberry

crowberry

butterwort

round-leaved sundew

bog asphodel

bog cotton

bog myrtle

yellow saxifrage

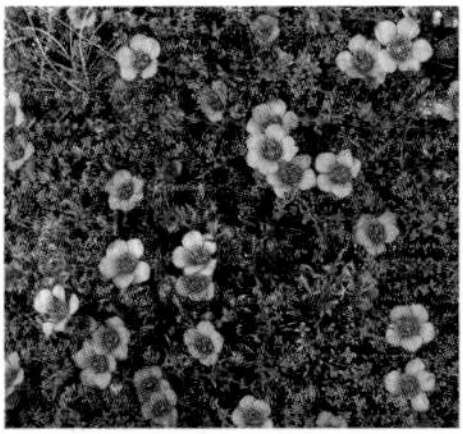

purple saxifrage

common spotted orchid

polytrichum commune

fir clubmoss

roseroot

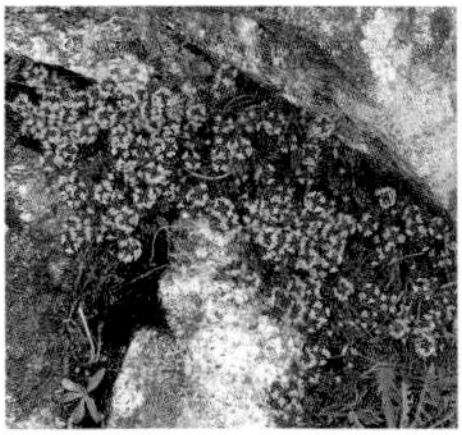

thyme

thrift

moss campion

alpine lady's mantle

heath milkwort

eyebright

Flora & Fauna

germander speedwell

grass of parnassus

common dog violet

selfheal

lesser celandine

greater stitchwort

primrose

Scottish bluebell (harebell)

wood sorrel

devil's-bit scabious

ramsons (wild garlic)

wood anemone

scots pine

rowan (in flower)

prostrate juniper

ptarmigan (male)

ptarmigan (female)

viviparous lizard

toad

common frog

golden-ringed dragonfly

scotch argus

emperor moth caterpillar

northern eggar moth caterpillar

Using this Guidebook

Route Maps & Mapping

Route maps accompanying the walks are drawn from out of copyright one inch Ordnance Survey (OS) mapping and half inch Bartholomew mapping, supplemented by in-the-field GPS tracks, and personal observation.

These route maps are only sketch maps and walkers are advised to purchase the up-to-date Ordnance Survey Landranger (1:50,000) or Explorer (1:25,000) scale maps for the walks. The relevant OS Landranger map for each walk is indicated by 'OS L56' etc in the information panel <www.ordnancesurvey.co.uk>.

Scottish-based Harvey maps produce a handy-sized Loch Lomond & The Trossachs National Park Outdoor Atlas (LLTOA in the information panel), which covers the whole park. This atlas uses data from their 1:25,000 scale mapping reduced in size, but not in detail, to 1:40,000 and represents excellent value for money <www.harvey maps.co.uk>.

Map Symbols

- P Car park or layby
- P Other parking
- ▲ Munro summit
- ▲ Corbett summit
- ▲ Graham summit
- ▲ Other summit
- Golf course

Route Symbols

- Route on path
- Route on pathless hillside
- Road
- Route along road
- Track
- Route along track
- Other path
- Optional extension

- routes on roads generally follow pavements or verges.
- tracks include all non-tarmac surfaces (farm and forest tracks), and All Terrain Vehicle (ATV) tracks on open hillsides.
- 'pathless' hillsides are often criss-crossed by paths created by sheep, deer, cattle or goats.

Access

The Land Reform (Scotland) Act 2003 grants everyone the right to be on most land and inland water for recreation, providing they act responsibly. These rights and responsibilities are explained in the Scottish Access Code <www.outdooraccess-scotland.com>.

- take personal responsibility for your own actions and act safely;
- respect people's privacy and peace of mind;
- help land managers and others to work safely and effectively;
- care for your environment and take your litter home;
- keep your dog under proper control;
- take extra care if you're organising an event or running a business

Grades & Times

The following grades have been used.

- **Easy**: Mostly low level waymarked routes on level terrain.
- **Easy / Moderate**: Generally on good paths but with inclines or rougher terrain in some places.
- **Moderate**: Mostly on paths, but requiring more stamina either due to length, terrain or steeper ground.
- **Moderate / Strenuous**: Longer

MUNROS: List of 284 peaks over 914.4m / 3000ft. Compiled by Sir Hugh Munro in 1891

CORBETTS: List of 219 peaks between 762m / 2500ft and 914m / 2999ft. Compiled by J Rooke Corbett in the 1930s

GRAHAMS: List of 224 peaks between 610m / 2000ft and 761m / 2499ft. Named after Fiona Graham

walks on paths over mixed terrain, or shorter hillwalks on paths or pathless hillside.

- **Strenuous**: Ascents of high hills via good paths, or less well-travelled lower peaks, often over pathless hillside.

Grading walks is very subjective and the amount of uphill ascent isn't the only factor in the equation. Distance and terrain must also be taken into account when choosing a walk.

Time is also subjective and influenced by factors including fitness, terrain, vertical ascent, steepness and weather. Timings are for round trips but do NOT include stops for lunch, rests or admiring the view.

Equipment & Weather

Stout footwear with a good tread is advisable for all walks, as many paths are on natural surfaces of earth or rock and can be wet and slippery.

Scotland's summer weather can vary significantly from place to place and from hour to hour. Waterproofs and warm clothing are recommended, especially above the treeline and on hillwalks. Adequate food and water should also be taken.

A map and compass and the ability to use them are essential for all walks above the treeline, where an unexpected reduction in visibility may result in serious disorientation. GPS units are useful but unless pre-programmed or used in good visibility, they can only tell you where you are and where you have come from, not where you need to go. Mobile telephones also have their uses but signal coverage is patchy in the glens.

Weather forecasting is not easy, but the following websites are worthwhile.

<www.mwis.org.uk> (Mountain Weather Information Service)
<www.metcheck.com>
<www.bbc.co.uk/weather>

BBC tv forecasts can be accessed via terrestrial and satellite services.

Midges & Ticks

Like most upland areas in the UK, Scotland suffers from midges. They are usually worst on warm, damp, overcast days and at dusk, but can be held at bay with various repellents.

Sheep and deer ticks are also prevalent in heather and long grass. Using repellent and wearing trousers tucked into socks will lessen the risk. Ticks can carry Lyme disease and checking for bites after a day's walking is important. For more information visit <www.lymediseaseaction.org.uk>

Travel

General: Traveline Scotland <www.travelinescotland.com>
Bus: Scottish City Link (08705 505050) <www.citylink.co.uk>
Rail & Bus: Scotrail, First <www.firstgroup.com>

Accommodation

Tourist Information Centres provide booking services, as does **visitscotland** (0845 22 55 121), <www.visitscotland.com>
Independent Hostels: <www.hostel-scotland.co.uk>
Scottish Youth Hostels: <www.syha.org.uk>
Campsites: <www.scottishcampingguide.com>

Balloch & Luss

Luss village

Balloch at the southern tip of Loch Lomond is the gateway to the National Park, and home to the Park headquarters. The main interest here is the Lomond Shores complex which combines shops, department store and outdoor market with an aquarium, National Park visitor centre, assorted recreational facilities and a fantastic view across the loch to Ben Lomond. The paddle steamer Maid of the Loch is berthed nearby and is easily visited, as is the refurbished 1906 steam winch built to haul boats from the loch. Lomond Shores attracts a range of visitors from tourist coaches to day trippers and while there is a pleasant ramble round the wooded point at the back of the National Park Gateway Centre, the extensive car park can also be utilised for more satisfying walks. **Balloch Castle Country Park** [1] leaves Lomond Shores and crosses east over the River Leven to the network of waymarked paths through the parkland surrounding this 19th century country house. **Stoneymollan** [2] goes westwards from Lomond Shores, following an old Right of Way onto the high moorland separating Loch Lomond from the River Clyde.

Ben Bowie [3] straddles the geological border between Highland and Lowland – the Highland Boundary Fault. The route to the summit starts from the B831 at the northern end of

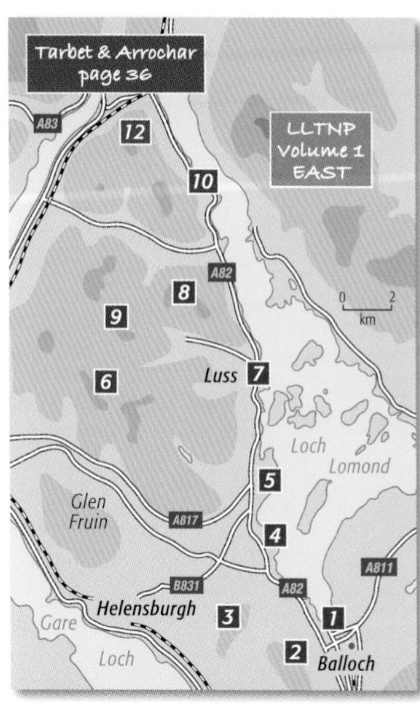

this moorland and is more of a hillwalk than a ramble, but worth the effort for the fine views over Loch Lomond. **Midross** [4] and **Ross Park** [5] offer pleasant lochside walks of a more rambly nature on waymarked paths through the lochside golf courses north of Balloch.

The remaining five walks lie north of the Highland Boundary Fault and offer a taste of routes in the following chapters. **Beinn Chaorach** [6], **Mid Hill** [8] and **Beinn Eich** [9] are three of the best summits in the Luss Hills, approached from Glen Fruin and Glen Luss.

Luss Village [7] and **Firkin Point** [10] return to the lochside. The walk round Luss explores the old slate quarries round the village and the lochside meadows and is suited to a lazy day. Firkin Point uses the old lochside road, where the generally car-free tarmac surface is perfect for wheelchairs and buggies.

GETTING THERE

Road: *From Glasgow & Edinburgh – M8, A82. From Stirling – A811, A82*

Train: *Scotrail from Glasgow Central (08457 484950), <www.firstgroup.com>*

Bus: *See pages 10 & 11*

TOWNS & VILLAGES

Balloch: *Supermarkets, hotels, restaurants, cafes, public toilets, banks, petrol stations, taxis, bicycle hire, Loch Lomond boat hire*

Luss: *Shops, hotels, restaurant, cafe, public toilets, bicycle hire, cruises and boat hire*

TOURIST INFORMATION CENTRES (TIC)

Balloch: *Gateway Centre at Lomond Shores (08707 200 631)*

Balloch: *Balloch Road (08707 200 607)*

NATIONAL PARK CENTRES & FACILITIES

Balloch: *Gateway Centre at Lomond Shores (08707 200 631)*

Luss: *Main car park (01389 722120)*

Firkin Point: *Car park, public toilets; closed during winter*

ACCOMMODATION

Centred on Balloch, Luss and Loch Lomond west shore, but widespread hotel and bed and breakfast. Campsites at Balloch and Luss. See also pages 10 & 11

1 Lomond Shores & Balloch Castle

Exploring Loch Lomond's southern shore

Ben Lomond and the Maid of the Loch

With its extensive free parking, the Lomond Shores complex at Balloch is a good starting point for walkers exploring the southern end of Loch Lomond. From here, linking paths can be followed to Balloch Castle Country Park and the Right of Way via **Stoneymollan** [2] to Cardross near Helensburgh.

From the car park walk north past the glass fronted National Park Gateway Centre towards the shopping mall and follow the lochside promenade round past Drumkinnon Tower and the Sealife Aquarium to Drumkinnon Bay.

Just beyond the adventure playground turn right at the junction signposted Maid of the Loch and Steam Winch House and follow the path to a roundabout. Cross straight over the road into parkland beside the River Leven where assorted paths lead south to the main road at Sweeny's Cruises. Follow the main road left over Balloch Bridge and continue to the park gates at South Lodge and a sign for Balloch Castle Country Park.

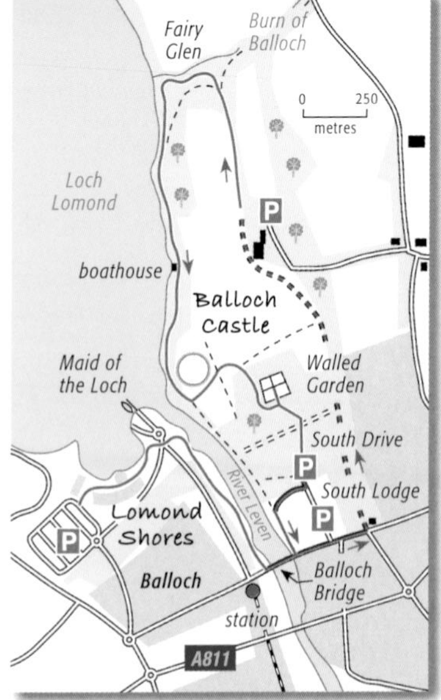

The South Drive leads through woodland then parkland to Balloch Castle and views across Loch Lomond. The

START & FINISH: *Red car park, Lomond Shores, Balloch*

DISTANCE: *7km; 4.25 miles*

TIME: *2hrs*

MAP: *OS 56; Harvey LLTOA*

TERRAIN: *Tracks and paths; mostly waymarked*

GRADE: *Easy*

castle was built in 1808 for wealthy Glasgow businessman John Buchanan, utilising some of the stone from the old castle at the mouth of the River Leven abandoned by the Earls of Lennox in the late 1300s. The castle and its 200 acres of lochside grounds and gardens were bought in the 1900s by Glasgow Corporation, to allow the public much needed access to the lochside and found a new popularity among day-trippers from the city. The condition of both grounds and castle deteriorated in the latter years of the 20th century, but with the formation of the Loch Lomond & The Trossachs National Park in 2002, Balloch Castle is regaining some of its past glory with path improvements and general refurbishment.

Continue past the front of the castle and the Chinese Garden and follow the tarmac path as it starts to descend through woodland to just after a bench on the right. Here a smaller path leads off right to the Burn of Balloch and the Fairy Glen, following them down to rejoin the main path at the bottom.

The route then follows the lochside passing an adventure playground and a boathouse, to arrive at the mouth of the River Leven. On the left lies the site of the old castle and an interpretation board. Little remains save for the raised foundations and the long-dry moat.

Soon after returning to the track, turn left onto a sometimes muddy path which crosses the parkland below the house and follow it over a track to gain a grassier path ascending to the South Drive. The woodland on the right hides the castle's old kitchen garden. At the next opportunity turn right onto a prepared path and continue round the walled garden to the arched entrance. Substantially restored in 2005, this comtemplative spot is a hard place to leave.

Exit the garden straight ahead to a rough track, then turn left to Moss of Balloch car park and pass through it to the edge of the recreation ground where a road leads right down to the River Leven walkway. Follow it left back to the main road at Balloch Bridge.

The old kitchen garden at Balloch Castle

2 Stoneymollan

Over the moor to the Cross Stone

Approaching Stoneymollan Muir

West of Balloch, on the very edge of the National Park, a ridge of high ground separates Loch Lomond from the River Clyde. The northern end is marked by the high point of **Ben Bowie** [3], but further south the ridge is characterised by open moorland.

This walk follows the first section of an old Right of Way from Loch Lomond to Cardross on the River Clyde, which starts as a beautiful beech-lined track with extensive views across Loch Lomond, then ascends to pass over the ridge at its lowest point; the Cross Stone on Stoneymollan Muir.

From the south-westerly corner of the Lomond Shores car park follow the tarmac path out to the old A82 (now a no through road) and turn left towards Balloch. Follow the road past a ruined mansion in parkland on the right, to a Scottish Rights of Way and Access Society signpost at Lower Stoneymollan Road, indicating a Public Footpath to Cardross.

Go up this tarmac road up past Drumkinnon Farm and Glendale Kennels and cross a footbridge over the new A82 bypass, to gain an access road. Ascend through woodland, still signposted Cardross, with fine views across to Balloch Castle and Loch Lomond. At the highest house the road ends at an access gate from where a track and firm, rocky footpath lead out onto the moor.

The views continue to improve as the path, now more of a grassy track, ascends steadily to reach the high crest of the ridge and a conifer plantation on the National Park boundary. The Cross Stone lies by the fence to the right of the gate and is thought to have formed the plinth for a cross, although doubt was cast on this as early as the 1890s and it is unlikely we shall ever know.

START & FINISH: *Red car park, Lomond Shores, Balloch*

DISTANCE: *7km; 4.25 miles*

TIME: *2hrs 15mins*

MAP: *OS 56; Harvey LLTOA*

TERRAIN: *Roads, tracks and paths; muddy in places*

GRADE: *Easy / Moderate*

WALK 1
Lomond Shores
& Balloch Castle

FOOTPATH TO
CARDROSS
6·5Km

Cameron Home Farm
Cameron House
Loch Lomond
A82
Stoneymollan
Lomond Shores
cross stone
230m
Upper Stoneymollan
Drumkinnon Farm
Balloch Station
A811
Bromley Muir
Farmhouse B&B
0 250 metres

Go through the gate and descend through the conifers, muddy in places, and over a forest road to where the woodland ends with southerly views over the River Clyde to Port Glasgow. A return can be made from here, or the Right of Way can be continued, again muddy in places, to a right turn at a T-junction above Blackthird farm. This track re-enters the forest and becomes the road crossed earlier, to complete a circular route (add 1km, 0.75 mile).

On the return route, turn right onto the access road half way down (sign-posted Farmhouse B&B), then immediately left onto a well worn path into the woodland, and follow it down past a waterfall, to exit onto the road at the bottom. Turn left and ascend slightly to regain the footbridge over the A82.

Balloch from the Stoneymollan track

3 Ben Bowie

Fine views of Loch Lomond from the Yellow Hill

Gouk Hill from Loch Lomond

Ben Bowie pokes its head from the grassy moorland at the southern end of the Luss Hills and it's name has nothing to do with rock stars or knife-wielding American frontiersmen. In his book *Scottish Hill Names*, Peter Drummond suggests that Bowie is actually an Anglicisation of the Gaelic word buidhe, meaning yellow, although Ben Bowie's eastern flanks are nowadays covered with forestry, making it more green than yellow for most of the year. It's a very pleasant hill offering relatively straightforward access to fine views over Loch Lomond.

Limited off-road parking can be found in woodland on the south side of the B832 at the start of a track (NS 842 327). Approaching from Loch Lomond, this is just before the Reduce Speed Now Bends sign. Care is needed as the B832 is busy and the parking is easily missed. Alternatively, a cycle path running alongside the road can be used to access the track from a farm road on the south side of the B832, at NS 335 846. When approaching from Loch Lomond this is just after the farm at Callendoun and before the bridge.

Go through the gate and follow the track, initially through woodland and then open ground with views across Glen Fruin to Beinn Tharsuinn and **Beinn Chaorach** [6]. A second gate gives access to conifer woodland flanked by silver birch and leads to a Y-junction. Veer right and shortly after the junction a wide firebreak containing a burn crosses the track offering views over Loch Lomond. Ascend a well-worn path left of the burn, initially through heather, then grass and bracken, to the top of the firebreak which appears barred by conifers. Pass through what is actually only a thin strip of trees to gain another firebreak which contours rightwards round the hillside, and has a clear path along its top edge.

START & FINISH: *Off-road parking on the B832 to Helensburgh*

DISTANCE: *8km; 5 miles*

TIME: *2hrs 30mins*

MAP: *OS 56; Harvey LLTOA*

TERRAIN: *Tracks, paths and pathless hillside; rough and wet in places*

GRADE: *Moderate*

A short distance along this firebreak on the left, a tunnel has been cut through the forest. Follow this with care to exit out onto the open hillside. If this does not appeal, then the firebreak can be followed rightwards and the open hillside ascended to the same point.

The summit area, marked by a few stones, lies to the south and offers fantastic views west to Helensburgh and the Clyde and north to the Luss Hills. Descend due south from here to a fence and follow it leftwards, avoiding some of the thicker areas of bracken further to the left. Care is needed here as the fence is very close by and topped with barbed wire and the ground is rough in places.

Fairly soon a clearer sheep path leads beside the fence to a gate and stile, from where a faint path leads leftwards alongside an old wall to gain the continuation of the access track from the road. Turn right and follow the track towards Gouk Hill, the small tree-surrounded knoll to the right. Go right where the track forks, descending past a small pond on the left to arrive at a bend. A narrow opening in the forest ahead reveals a path leading to a wider clearing through the trees.

Follow this to the open top of the hill and a fine view over Loch Lomond and its islands. Return towards the clearing utilised on the ascent, but just before it, a cleared tunnel on the right leads down, steeply at first, to a burn, then ascends again to a track.

Cross straight over the track and ascend the heather hillside to the top of the next hill. Turn left and follow tracks past old limestone workings to regain the main track. Turn right and follow the track back to the road.

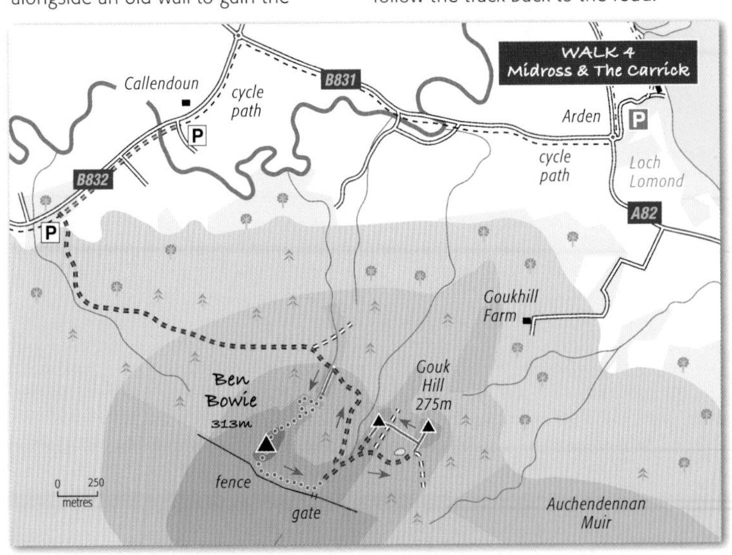

4 Midross & The Carrick

Golf, Bronze Age burials and Romans

Glen Fruin hills from Midross

Between Balloch and Luss the shores of Loch Lomond are dominated by golf courses, exclusive hotels and their attendant residential developments. The 2003 Land Reform Act gives responsible walkers the right to cross over all these courses, providing walkers keep off the greens and do not interfere with the game. In reality, speeding golf balls limit access, but for any golf course willing to make the effort, there is always enough space for walkers and golfers to co-exist without getting in the other's way.

The Carrick at Midross is one of the most recent golf course developments in this area and specifically caters for walkers and cyclists with a prepared and waymarked route right through the site, from the Colquhoun Gates on the A82 at Auchentullich, to the roundabout at Arden. Despite the unnatural landscape of cropped fairways, manicured greens and sandpits, the walk is surprisingly enjoyable, offering loch and mountain views and close proximity to a nature reserve among the marshy lochside lagoons. During the development, archaeological excavation unearthed Bronze Age cremation urns, Roman jewellery, an Iron Age settlement, Viking burials and post-medieval grain drying kilns; a remarkable 3,500 years of history in one small area.

From the southern end of the parking at the Colquhoun Gates (NS 352 867), follow the tarmac lane round into woodland where it becomes a track. Beyond the gate and access notice, the

START & FINISH: *Colquhoun Gates or Burnfoot car park on A82*

DISTANCE: *7km; 4.25 miles*

TIME: *2hrs*

MAP: *OS 56; Harvey LLTOA*

TERRAIN: *Waymarked roads, tracks and cycle paths*

GRADE: *Easy*

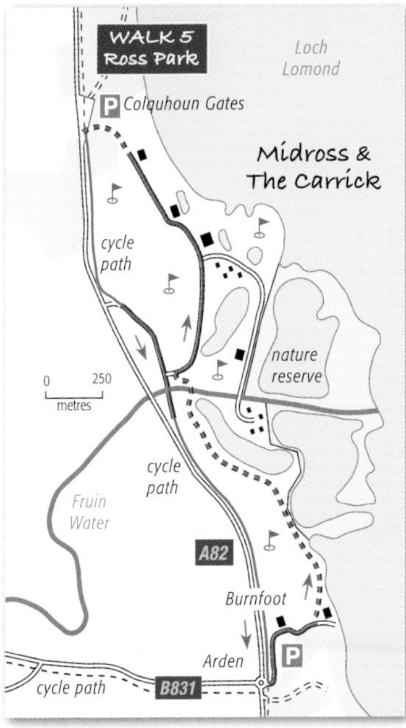

track continues south above the golf course, with views across to Ben Lomond, before descending past various buildings to join the access road, which is followed towards the golf course entrance. Turn left here and cross the bridge over the Fruin Water to pass through trees with pleasant views south to **Ben Bowie** [3].

The area alongside the nature reserve is slightly wilder and leads to a board-walk through the lochside marshes, and the access road to the Inchmurrin Island jetty at Burnfoot. From here a return can be made by the same route or via the cycle path alongside the A82. The cycle path is easily reached by following the access road past the public car park near Burnfoot Farm to the Arden roundabout, from where it can be followed back to the Colquhoun Gates, with a short diversion at the old bridge over the Fruin Water. This route is pleasant enough, but can be noisy when the road is very busy.

New bridge over the Fruin Water

5 Ross Park

Through the Colquhoun Gates to the Black Headland

Colquhoun Gates at Ross Park

Loch Lomond's most northerly golf course centres round the Georgian mansion of Rossdhu House, the former home of Clan Colquhoun of Luss. Now the home of Loch Lomond Golf Club, the estate can be traced back to the ruined Chapel of St Mary near the mansion, said to have been founded in the 12th century. The chapel used to house the famous Rossdhu Book of Hours. This medieval manuscript of Christian texts, psalms and prayers dates from the late 1400s and belonged to Elizabeth Dunbar, wife of Sir John Colquhoun of Luss. It now takes pride of place in the Central Library in Auckland, New Zealand <www.aucklandcitylibraries.com>.

The mansion house at Rossdhu (the Black Headland) was built in the 1770s for Sir James Colquhoun, who was also responsible for improvements to Ross Park and the imposing gates at the southern end of the estate. The mansion replaced a 15th century castle, and utilised much of its stone, although two walls of the castle remain standing. Ruins of a possibly even older castle can be found on the ancient man-made island, or crannog, of Eilean Rossdhu in the bay.

From the large car park at the Colquhoun Gates (NS 352 867) go through the white gate in the railings nearest the road to a Public Footpath sign and follow the track through broadleaf woodland. Rhododendron clearing has taken place all along the route improving access to the lochside and opening the views. Where the gravel track ends, gain a rougher track and path on the right, sticking to the edge of the woodland, with occasional waymarks and views north-east to Ben Lomond. Leave the track at a new gate, fence and marker post and take a diagonal route north-west through meadow to a fence and stile. Go left along the access road, then right onto a

START & FINISH: *Colquhoun Gates at Auchentullich on A82*

DISTANCE: *9km; 5.5 miles*

TIME: *2 hrs 30mins*

MAP: *OS 56; Harvey LLTOA*

TERRAIN: *Tracks, paths and cycle paths; some waymarking*

GRADE: *Easy*

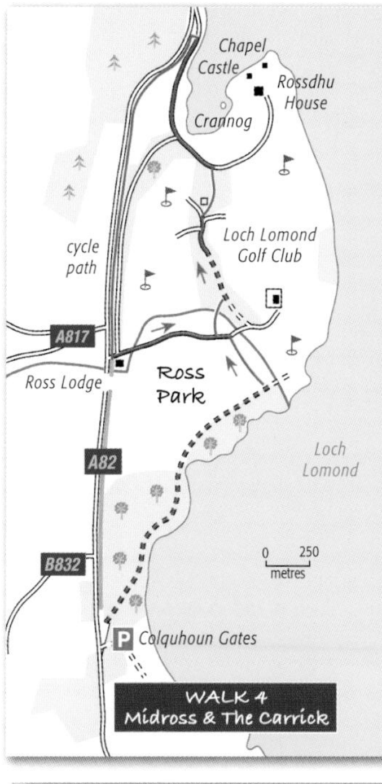

waymarked gravel path.

This crosses the river on a footbridge and through woodland to a track cross-roads. Turn left following the waymark, the old kitchen garden lies to the right, and the track turns to a tarmac access road through the golf course. Take the second turning on the left, the first leads down to a maintenance area, then almost immediately right, following waymarks to gain a track passing right of a dilapidated barn.

Pass through some woodland to the next junction and turn left onto the main access road at the edge of the bay, from where there are views over to Rossdhu House and the ruins of Rossdhu Castle. Follow the road to green wooden steps over the boundary wall, which accesses the cycle path alongside the A82.

The first section of the cycle path is separated from the road by trees, but from Ross Lodge the route is very exposed to traffic noise and a pleasanter return route is to re-enter the park at the lodge and retrace the outward route back to the gates.

Ben Lomond from Ross Park

6 Beinn Chaorach

The Highland edge above Glen Fruin

Beinn Chaorach

Above Glen Fruin and Glen Luss, the hills are generally rounded, grassy and well-tramped. The glens however, are surprisingly deep and steep-sided, creating summits of individual character and interest to the hillwalker.

Most of the upper glens can be accessed via farm tracks, but animal paths predominate from there, leaving route finding on the less-frequented hills to the individual. This is certainly the case with Beinn Chaorach, the most southerly of the high hills in this group.

Two roads pass through Glen Fruin, a traditional route along the floor of the glen and a newer upper road, the A817. This was built for MoD vehicles servicing the bases on Gare Loch and Loch Long and vehicles are not allowed to stop or park. Take the lower road through Glen Fruin to park west of Auchingaich in a large layby at the bottom of an old access road to Auchingaich Reservoir below Beinn Chaorach (NS 274 900). Go through the gate and follow the old access road up to the A817. Cross over with great care and follow the new access road to a stile and signpost to Glen Luss.

Go over and almost immediately leave the track for the pathless hillside on the right. Avoiding the initial boggy patches, ascend diagonally north-east with fine views west over Gare Loch and Loch Long, to arrive at the col between Auchingaich Hill and Beinn Tharsuinn. Head right to avoid the worst of the peat hags at the col and gain an ATV track leading to the summit of Beinn Tharsuinn, marked with a small cairn and fine views across to **Beinn Eich** [9], Glen Luss and more distant **Mid Hill** [8]. Follow the fence north, crossing to its right side to avoid the wettest section of the marshy col, then ascend

START & FINISH: *Layby west of Auchingaich, Glen Fruin*

DISTANCE: *9.5km; 6 miles*

TIME: *3hrs 30mins*

MAP: *OS 56; Harvey LLTOA*

TERRAIN: *Tracks, paths and pathless hillside*

GRADE: *Moderate / Strenuous*

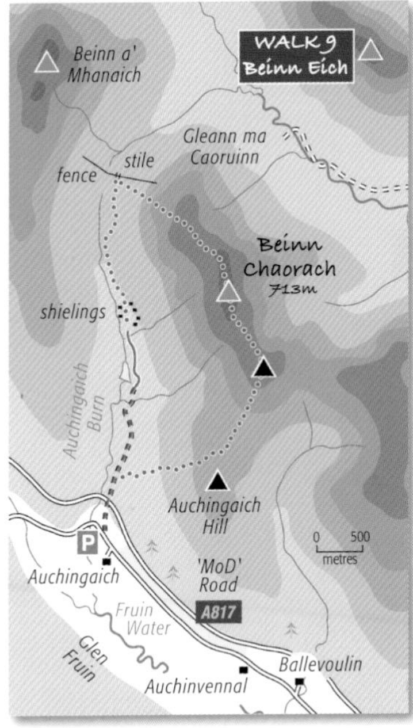

on a path beside the fence to the summit of Beinn Chaorach, where the fence separates the cairn from the trig point. Loch Lomond and Ben Lomond are now clear with the Arrochar Alps and distant Ben Cruachan further west.

The left side of the fence is followed down to the next col and over the north ridge of the hill, then west and down to the col between Beinn Chaorach and Beinn a' Mhanaich. As the col approaches, contour left (south-west) into the glen and follow the higher and drier ground above the Auchingaich Burn heading for the reservoir.

This route is a Right of Way with occasional waymark posts, although there is no path, and the going is a little rough, but fairly dry. An area of old shielings is reached before the reservoir, from where a path leads to a stile in the small conifer plantation east of the reservoir. Enter the plantation and head right to gain a good path which exits at the dam and the access road leading back to the start.

Ascending Auchingaich Hill

7 Luss Village

Sheep, slate and the Clearances

Luss village

This tiny planned village on Loch Lomond holds an important place in Highland history. In the mid-1700s blackface sheep were introduced to the hills of Glen Luss, one of the first locations in the country. Over the next century tenant farmers throughout the Highlands and Islands were steadily cleared from the land and replaced by more profitable sheep.

At Luss, they found work in the slate quarries, mills and surrounding oak woodlands. The legacy of this industry can be explored during this walk, which finishes with a stroll around the parish church and neat streets of the village planned in the 19th century by Sir James Colquhoun, 12th Baronet of Colquhoun and Luss.

From the car park walk out to the road and turn left, then right shortly after. Follow the dead-end road passing Luss Primary on the right and ascend steps to the wooden bridge over the A82 Luss bypass to the start of the Glen Luss road. Continue straight ahead then cross over the road to a new wooden gate and the signposted Quarry Path.

A gravelled path winds round and down through woodland interspersed with slate waste. The river soon makes its presence known as you descend to cross it on a new wooden bridge. The upturned slate strata is well-exposed in the banks and bed of the river at this point. Immediately after the bridge, ignore the right turning to the private house at Mill Cottage, and continue straight ahead past some large slate mounds to an information board. The path now rises above the river passing a weir and houses on the other side.

Pass under the A82 at the bridge and continue to exit onto the old road near

START & FINISH: *Luss village pay and display car park*

DISTANCE: *4km; 2.5 miles*

TIME: *1hr 15mins*

MAP: *OS 56; Harvey LLTOA*

TERRAIN: *Roads and paths; mostly waymarked*

GRADE: *Easy*

the fields used for the Luss Highland Games. Turn left and cross the road, then right at the next signpost to regain the path which is now on the other side of the river. Follow this round beside the river with views across open meadow to Glen Luss and **Beinn Dubh** [8], to arrive at a kissing gate and a road.

Turn immediately right and over a bridge into the meadowland of Luss Church Glebe. Follow the circular footpath round the meadow with views of the church spire with Ben Lomond behind. This path is being refurbished and may be boggy in places. At the north-eastern side of the glebe it is possible to explore paths through the woodland to gain the lochside, but care is needed as the paths are indistinct and marshy in places.

Cross back over the bridge and turn right to pass the church and continue past the Coach House cafe to a

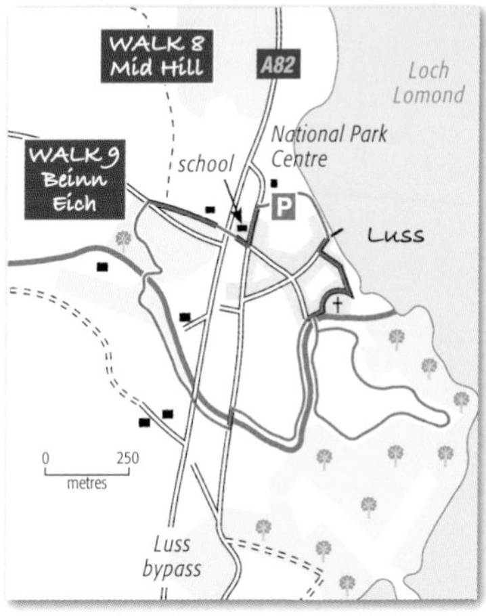

junction. Turn right and follow the road down towards the pier. Descend on the left down to the surprisingly sandy beach and follow it north to exit back at the car park.

Slate waste in the old quarries

8 Beinn Dubh & Mid Hill

A classic round above Glen Luss

Arrochar Alps from Beinn Dubh

Beinn Dubh's long south-east ridge rises straight from the village of Luss and offers spectacular views across Loch Lomond and its islands. Combining it with higher neighbour Mid Hill produces one of the most popular hillwalks in the area, offering a gradual ascent with panoramic views east over Loch Lomond and north to the Arrochar Alps and the distinctive pointed silhouette of **The Cobbler** [18].

The best starting place is the main pay and display car park in Luss. Turn left out of the car park, follow the road to Luss Primary School and turn right up a short section of road by the school. This is marked by a blacked-out road sign at the start stating 'Glen Luss No Through Road' and is part of the old Glen Luss road, now truncated by the new A82 bypass.

Ascend to the wooden bridge over the main road and cross over. On the other side, continue past the house on a gravel path through a new gate and turn immediately right off the main path. Cross the stile and ascend pasture to a new metal gate and stile from where a track leads through a small section of woodland and past a mobile phone mast to reach the top of the first bump on the ridge.

The noise of traffic on the A82 below is hard to ignore, but so is the view over the loch and across to Ben Lomond. The path now flattens out a bit and becomes a little wetter as a result, but this is soon lost as you start climbing again. Maintain a direct approach up the hillside ignoring paths off to the sides and join a fence, where more extensive views can be had down into Glen Luss on the left. The fence leads to the top of Beinn Dubh, crossing a stile en route.

Further on, the path is less well-defined as it passes through a small area of peat haggs in the col between the two hills, but soon starts again and

START & FINISH: *Luss village pay and display car park*

DISTANCE: *11.5km; 7 miles*

TIME: *4hrs*

MAP: *OS 56; Harvey LLTOA*

TERRAIN: *Roads and paths; boggy in places*

GRADE: *Moderate / Strenuous*

leads round to a cairn marking the summit of what is named point 657m on the Ordnance Survey map. For more than 30 years hillwalkers have known this point as Mid Hill, although the name technically refers to the smaller hump on the ridge immediately to the south.

From the summit continue south-west to the undeniable Mid Hill then follow the path down the steepish south-east ridge into Glen Striddle crossing a stile over a fence and continuing down to a gate in the wall below. From here veer right to the track and cross the gate to the Glen Luss road, which is followed back down to the bridge and Luss village.

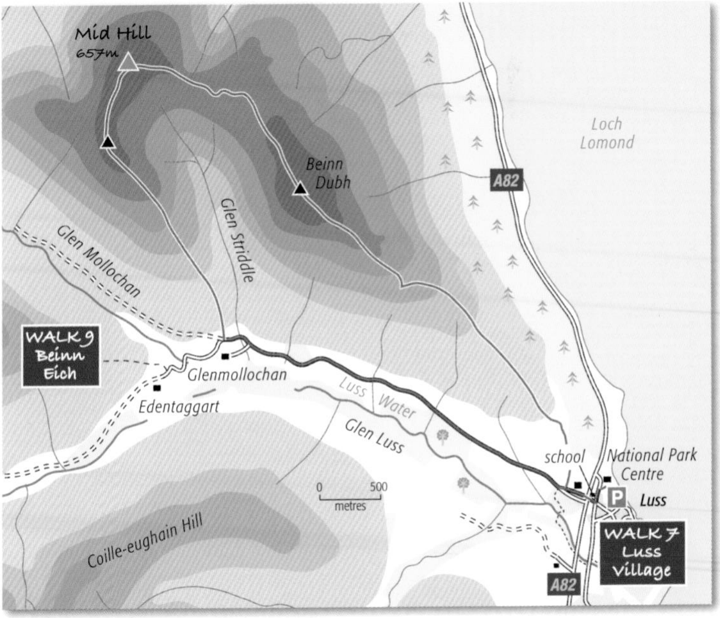

Mid Hill
657m
Beinn Dubh
Loch Lomond
A82
Glen Striddle
Glen Mollochan
WALK 9 Beinn Eich
Glenmollochan
Edentaggart
Luss Water
Glen Luss
school
National Park Centre
P
Luss
0 500 metres
Coille-eughain Hill
WALK 7 Luss Village
A82

9 Beinn Eich

Climbing the Mountain of the Horses

Beinn Eich and Glen Luss from the north

Viewed from the north-east or east, Beinn Eich (the mountain of the Horses) presents an impressively steep profile above Glen Luss. Despite this, an ascent is straightforward, for Beinn Eich is not the highest hill in the area and lies very close to the road. Route finding is not really a problem either. If in doubt, keep heading straight up!

However, there is very limited parking where the public road ends at Glenmollachan farm. Walking up Glen Luss from the village almost doubles the time and distance for the walk, although the road is quiet and the glen scenic. Appoaching via bicycle is also an option. The start of the Glen Luss road is steep, but it is less strenuous thereafter and the descent requires very little effort!

If walking from the village the best starting place is the main pay and display car park in Luss. Turn left out of the car park, follow the road to Luss Primary School and turn right up a short section of road by the school. This is marked by a blacked-out road sign at the start stating 'Glen Luss No Through Road' and is part of the old Glen Luss road, now truncated by the new A82 bypass.

Ascend to the wooden bridge over the main road and cross over, continuing past the house to the Glen Luss road and follow it past Glenmollochan Farm and on to Edentaggart where the road turns to a farm track. Before the farm, a stile and signpost on the right indicates the route to Glen Fruin, Glen na Caorainn and Beinn Eich straight ahead. Over a stile, an indistinct and marshy path leads across to a wall and a stile with a signpost to Glen na Caorainn and Glen Fruin. Ascend diagonally up and left to a hidden wooden stile and gate in

START & FINISH: *Luss village pay and display car park*

DISTANCE: *13.5km; 8.25 miles*

TIME: *4hrs 30mins*

MAP: *OS 56; Harvey LLTOA*

TERRAIN: *Roads, tracks and paths; some signposting*

GRADE: *Moderate / Strenuous*

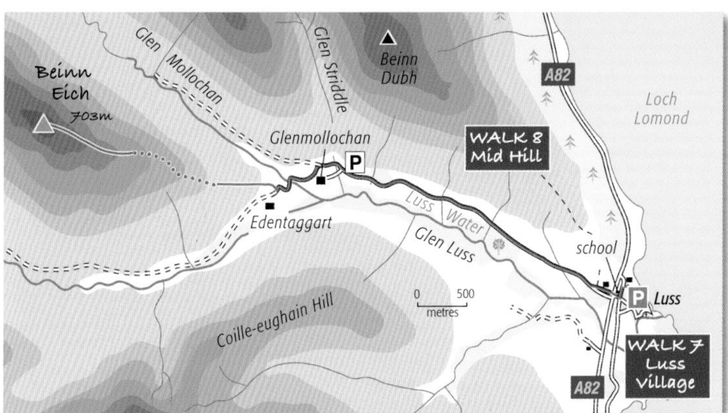

the wall above and cross over to the open hillside.

The path continues up and left to an area of bracken where an old track traverses below more extensive bracken before clearer ground is reached. Gain Beinn Eich's grassy south-east ridge up and to the right and follow it in an airy position high above Glen Luss to arrive at the lofty summit, marked with a cairn of mica schist and quartz stones.

From here a wide panorama can be enjoyed east and north over the Luss Hills to Loch Lomond and the Arrochar Alps and west to the hills of Ardgoil and Cowal. Return to Glen Luss by the outward route.

Glenmollochan Farm

Edentaggart and Loch Lomond from Beinn Eich

10 Firkin Point

Shingle beaches on the old lochside road

Ben Lomond from Firkin Point

This all-ability route utilises a long section of the old Loch Lomond road at Firkin Point, offering travellers the opportunity to stretch their legs and admire the views of Ben Lomond. The tarmac surface is also used by the cycle route beside the loch, so the walk can be extended beyond the old road as far as desired in either direction. Most however, will be happy to stick to the old road which offers sufficient exercise in itself. In places the surface is slowly being covered by a thick mat of grass, showing how fast nature takes over in the absence of cars.

The main car park is well signposted from the A82 between Inverbeg and Tarbet. From the car park walk to the lochside and turn left onto the old road, which is gated off from vehicles at this point. Follow the road north out of the gated section and on past houses and Firkin Toll House to enter the next gated section. This leads past Rubha Dubh and Rubha Bàn – the Black and White Headlands – to where it ends at the main road.

Retrace your steps to enter the car park and veer left to a path ascending into woodland on the small hillside east of the car park. The path runs above the old road for a short distance then descends to meet it at an oak leaf waymark post. This short stretch of path offers a pleasant change to the tarmac, but is also easily avoided by remaining on the old road.

This southern section is perhaps slightly more attractive being totally closed to vehicle traffic and offering access to small shingle beaches on the lochside. Beyond Rubha Mòr, the Big Headland, the old road narrows down to cycle width, signalling an end to the old road and time to retrace your steps to the car park.

Assorted signboards along the route describe the history, geography and geology of the surrounding landscape.

START & FINISH: *Firkin Point car park on A82 (closed in winter)*

DISTANCE: *9.5km; 6 miles*

TIME: *2hrs 15mins*

MAP: *OS 56; Harvey LLTOA*

TERRAIN: *Roads (mostly closed to traffic) and cycle paths; waymarks*

GRADE: *Easy*

Tarbet & Arrochar

A' Chrois, left, and Ben Lomond far right, from Beinn Ime

Ease of access and spectacular mountain scenery make Arrochar and its famous 'Alps' one of the most popular destinations for walkers and tourists west of Loch Lomond. Star of the show is the spectacular rocky peak of **The Cobbler** [18] at the head of Loch Long. To its east lies the larger, higher and almost as popular **Beinn Narnain** [17]. Despite this popularity, it is still possible to escape the crowds as the described route shows. Arrochar also offers much for walkers wishing to stick to the glens, from the pleasant **Succoth Loop** [15] to the longer round of **Glen Loin** [16].

Immediately east of Glen Loin, the small hill of **Cruach Tairbeirt** [13] is easily accessed from the village of Tarbet to its south, as is the higher **Ben Reoch** [12], further south again. Also accessible from Tarbet is the short but delightful forest walk at **Tarbet Isle** [11]. To the west, an interesting route links **Tarbet to Arrochar** [14] via tracks and paths on the north and south sides of the glen which connects them.

Ardgarten Visitor Centre lies at the foot of Glen Croe on the north shore of Loch Long, south-west of Arrochar, and gives access to an interesting walk round the former cycle route of the **Cat Craig Loop** [19]. This forest walk

utilises access tracks and offers fine views over Loch Long, with a lochshore finish. The visitor centre also provides access south along the loch to the Coilessan Glen. From here a relatively straightforward ascent can be made to the top of **Cnoc Coinnich** [20] for views across Ardgoil to Lochgoilhead and the hills of Cowal.

To the north, Glen Croe and Glen Kinglas provide the starting points for three more excellent hillwalks. **Ben Donich** [21] and **Beinn an Lochain** [22] are both easily accessed from the 'Rest and be thankful' pass between these two deep glens and offer interesting routes to well-defined summits. **Beinn Chorranach** [23] is rather neglected in favour of nearby Beinn Ìme, despite being a well-proportioned summit and higher than The Cobbler. The approach via Glen Kinglass and the old croft at Abyssinia, coupled with extensive views to the surrounding high peaks and a certain solitude, make it a hill well worth seeking out.

Like other areas in this guidebook which are located on the west shore of Loch Lomond, Tarbet and Arrochar are easily reached by train from Glasgow's Central Station.

GETTING THERE

Road: *From Glasgow & Edinburgh – M8, A82. From Stirling – A811, A82*

Train: *Scotrail from Glasgow Central (08457 484950), <www.firstgroup.com>*

Bus: *See pages 10 & 11*

TOWNS & VILLAGES

Tarbet: *Hotels, restaurant, cafes, public toilets, Loch Lomond cruises*

Arrochar: *Shops, hotels, restaurants, cafes, bank, petrol station*

TOURIST INFORMATION CENTRES (TIC)

Tarbet: *Opposite Tarbet Hotel (08707 200 623); Apr – Oct*

Ardgarten: *Glen Croe (08707 200 606); Apr – Oct*

NATIONAL PARK CENTRES & FACILITIES

Ardgarten: *Forestry Commission Scotland Visitor Centre, Glen Croe (01301 702432)*

ACCOMMODATION

Extensive hotel and bed and breakfast options available in the Tarbet & Arrochar area. Campsite at Ardgarten. See also pages 10 & 11

11 Tarbet Isle

A short but delightful forest walk

Tarbet Isle wood

North of Tarbet the narrow A82 hugs the shore of Loch Lomond offering limited opportunities to stop and explore the lochside woodlands until Inveruglas is reached. This short walk is one of the exceptions, although the Tarbet Isle car park is easily missed from the main road. Accordingly, the walk is best approached from the large car park in Tarbet, located on the lochside opposite the Tarbet Hotel and accessed from the A82 (NN 319 045). From the car park exit to the Tarbet Hotel, turn right and follow the road out of the village. There is a pavement on the right for most of the way, but as the village ends this fades. Cross over left with care and after a very short distance a tarmac path starts beside the road and leads to the access road to Tarbet Isle woodland.

Tarbet Isle itself lies just off the shore and is easily seen from the lochside opposite the entrance to the wood. Ascend the track to a gate and parking area and continue straight ahead on a path offering views across the loch to Ben Lomond and south to **Ben Reoch** [**12**]. The forestry here is mostly mature pine woodland interspersed with broadleaf and offers a fine back-drop to the loch on a sunny day.

The path leads north to bring you round to the Bonnie Braes tearoom, before turning back on itself and climbing to a high point. The wall to the right marks the boundary of the old military road which ascended directly from Tarbet, before dropping back to the lochside. From this high point the path descends through pine forest to join the access track.

START & FINISH: *Lochside car park on A82, opposite Tarbet Hotel*

DISTANCE: *5km; 3 miles*

TIME: *1hr 30mins*

MAP: *OS 56; Harvey LLTOA*

TERRAIN: *Roads and waymarked paths; muddy in places*

GRADE: *Easy*

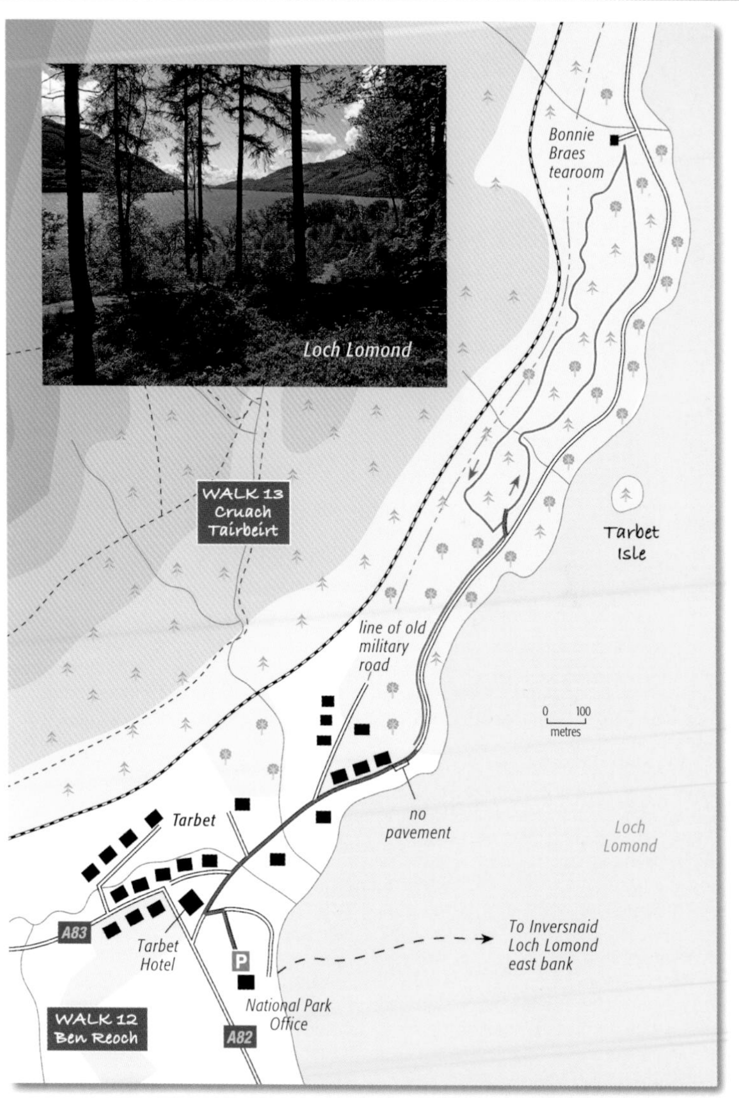

12 Ben Reoch

Panoramic views from an unfrequented summit

Ben Reoch from Tarbet

Although significantly smaller and less dramatic than neighbouring peaks such as The Cobbler, this is a satisfying hillwalk with fine views to the Arrochar summits and across the loch to Ben Lomond.

Park at the large car park in Tarbet, located on the lochside opposite the Tarbet Hotel and accessed from the A82 (NN 319 045). Ben Reoch is the hill immediately to the south, overlooking the hotel. The going is generally good although there are no paths and you should be prepared for some wet ground in places. Follow the pavement of the A83 north then west towards Arrochar and Tarbet station, to the third metal gate on the left opposite Ballyhennan Crescent and directly opposite the bus stop.

Go through the gate and follow the tarmac road up towards a water treatment plant with a perimeter fence. Turn right onto the track towards the house at Stuckdhu (or Stuckiedhu) and skirt the fence to gain the open hillside.

Ascend this steadily to the broad ridge ahead and follow it to a more level area. From here the route continues in a south-easterly direction to gain the better-defined ridge between the Loch Lomond and Arrochar faces of the mountain, passing over a number of unexpectedly steep false summits. These eventually lead to more level ground before a final pull to the summit of the lower northerly top.

Pass two large cairns to gain an old wall which leads directly to the summit cairn and open views south to **Beinn**

START & FINISH: *Lochside car park on A82, opposite Tarbet Hotel*

DISTANCE: *9.5km; 6 miles*

TIME: *3hrs 30mins*

MAP: *OS 56; Harvey LLTOA*

TERRAIN: *Roads, tracks and pathless hillside*

GRADE: *Moderate / Strenuous*

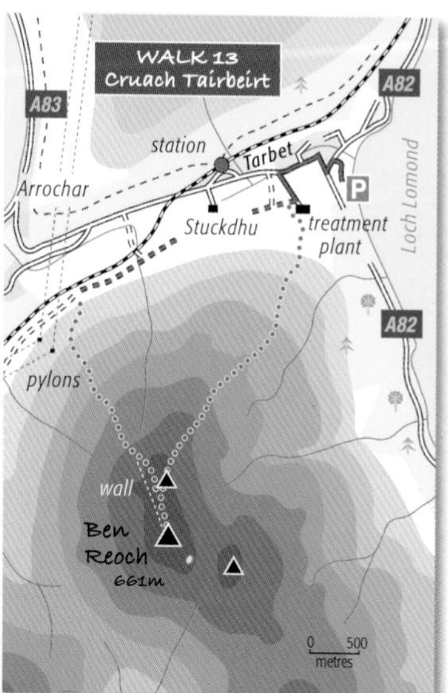

Eich [9] and east to Ben Lomond. **Cruach Tairbeirt** [13], a constant companion on the walk, lies immediately to the north and **Ben Vorlich** [46] can now be seen in the distance beyond. To the west the craggy outline of **The Cobbler** [18] dominates the view.

From the summit retrace your route to the wall and continue following it until it ends just west of the lower top. Continue descending straight ahead towards Arrochar below, avoiding the slightly rockier hillside further to the right, to arrive at a track.

Turn right and follow the track above the railway, with Arrochar and Loch Long below. The track offers good views of The Cobbler, and the craggy profiles of **Beinn Narnain & A' Chrois** [17], before you pass a sheep pen and Stuckdhu to arrive back at the access road.

Cruach Tairbeirt from Ben Reoch

13 Cruach Tairbeirt

The most popular small hill in the area

Cruach Tairbeirt
from Loch Lomond

Cruach is Gaelic for heap, hump or stack and while Tarbet Heap doesn't sound too inspiring, Stack Tarbet does sound worthy of further investigation. This isn't a very high hill, but the views down Loch Lomond and Loch Long are exceptional. Despite the height and the waymarked paths it is very much a hillwalk, so come prepared for boggy ground.

Park in the car park at the old church in Tarbet – currently the Ben Lomond Restaurant (NN 313 044). Walk up Station Road towards Arrochar and Tarbet station, pass below the railway and continue to a path junction. Follow the footpath right, signposted Cruach Loop. Ascend a short distance, cross the burn and descend the other side to follow a path parallel to and above the railway line.

Cross a footbridge, then ascend

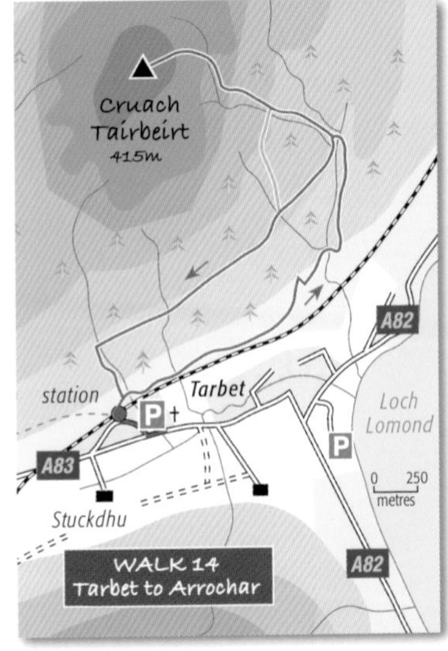

START & FINISH: *Ben Lomond Restaurant car park on A83, Tarbet*

DISTANCE: *6.5km; 4 miles*

TIME: *2hrs 30mins*

MAP: *OS 56; Harvey LLTOA*

TERRAIN: *Paths; some waymarks, boggy and rough in places*

GRADE: *Easy / Moderate*

beside the burn to arrive at a second bridge, with a picnic table above. About 12 paces up from the bridge leave the main path for a fainter path on the right which leads, on and off, up through open woodland beside the burn to arrive at a forestry break coming in from the left. This break could be ascended from further along the main path, but is one of the largest quagmires in the Southern Highlands and best avoided.

A firm, well-worn path continues to an excellent track which leads out onto the open hillside where it becomes a bit wetter and rougher. A final ascent through steepish heather leads to the trig point and fine views south across the loch to Ben Lomond and north to the impressively craggy east face of **A' Chrois** [17].

Return by the same route, taking particular care when descending the steep heather and follow the burn back to the main path. Turn right and follow the main path back round in a loop to the start. If the weather is against the chance of getting any summit views, then the loop path alone gives firm and generally dry walking.

Cruach loop walk, Tairbeirt wood

Ben Lomond from Cruach Tairbeirt

14 Tarbet to Arrochar

Loch Lomond to Loch Long by a low level route

A' Chrois, left, Arrochar and Long Long

This walk utilises paths and tracks on either side of the glen between Tarbet and Arrochar to give a satisfying low level walk with fine mountain views to the Arrochar Alps and Ben Lomond. The track can be quite wet and there are a couple of rough sections, although the going is generally good. Suitable footwear is recommended.

Park in the car park at the old church in Tarbet – currently the Ben Lomond Restaurant (NN 313 044). Walk up Station Road towards Arrochar and Tarbet station, pass below the railway and continue to a path junction, as for **Cruach Tairbeirt** [13]. Turn left, sign-posted Arrochar 3.6km (2.25 miles), and follow the undulating path through conifers then broadleaf woodland to emerge on rougher open hillside facing **Ben Reoch** [12] to the south. Pass below the power lines and swing round north with fine views across Arrochar and Loch Long to a path junction.

Turn left, the **Succoth Loop** [15] continues straight ahead, and descend steeply to emerge on the main road in Arrochar. Turn left past the well marking Queen Victoria's 1887 Jubilee, then cross over and follow the road south alongside Loch Long. Follow the road right at the junction before the Arrochar Hotel, continuing beside Loch Long.

Just before the church turn left into Church Road and follow it to a children's play area on the left before houses. Cross the play area towards the conifer woodland where a small footbridge gives access to a path up a wide forest ride through the trees. Break off right near the top and cross a sleeper bridge to gain a path, then a

START & FINISH: *Ben Lomond Restaurant car park on A83, Tarbet*

DISTANCE: *6.5km; 4 miles*

TIME: *2hrs 15mins*

MAP: *OS 56, 56; Harvey LLTOA*

TERRAIN: *Roads, tracks and paths; muddy and rough in places*

GRADE: *Easy*

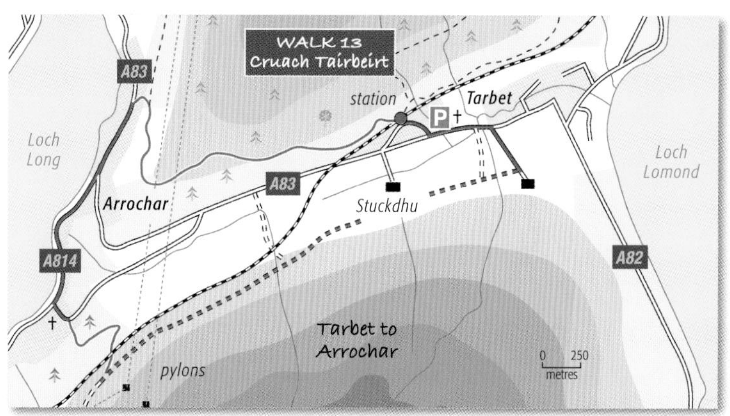

track beyond it and follow the track to a small 'cattle creep' bridge under the railway line.

Pass through the gate and ascend a rocky and wet path to open hillside and a track. Turn left and follow the track east below the electricity pylons with views up to **The Cobbler** [18] and Cruach Tairbeirt. The track leads past sheep pens and the house at Stuckdhu to join the tarmac road utilised as access for Ben Reoch. Follow the road down to the main road, then turn left back to the car park.

Arrochar Parish Church below Ben Reoch

15 Succoth Loop

A short stroll around Arrochar

Sunset on Loch Long

Arrochar is well served with an assortment of footpaths offering something for everyone. This route combines waymarked forest paths with quiet access roads to provide a pleasant countryside stroll. There are some uphill sections, but the paths are good and the effort is worth making for the views over Loch Long.

The walk can be started from either of the pay and display car parks at the head of Loch Long. From the most westerly of the car parks – they are linked by a walkway – gain the access path to **The Cobbler** [18] and zigzag up the hillside to the upper track and views over Loch Long.

Ben Lomond above Arrochar

Turn right and follow the forest track, keeping right where it divides, and descend above Succoth to lower Glen Loin. Turn right in the glen and follow

START & FINISH: *Loch Long car parks on A83, Arrochar*

DISTANCE: *6.5km; 4 miles*

TIME: *2hrs 15mins*

MAP: *OS 56; Harvey LLTOA*

TERRAIN: *Roads, tracks and paths; some waymarking*

GRADE: *Easy*

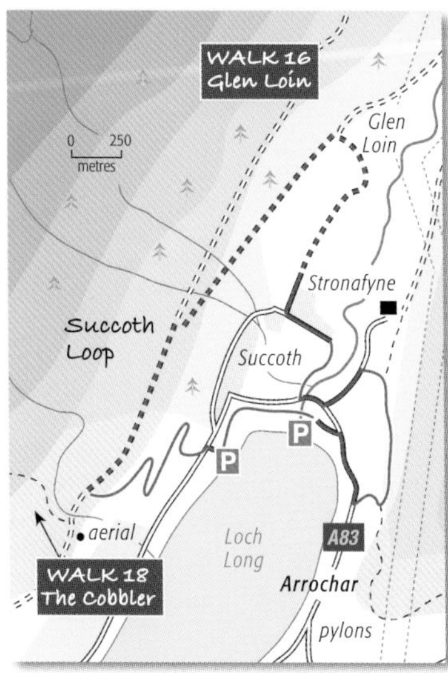

the access track through pasture towards the houses of Succoth, with views ahead to **Ben Reoch** [12] and Loch Long and back up Glen Loin to **Ben Vorlich** [46].

Turn left at the T-junction in Succoth and follow the road down to a path on the right which leads back to the main road near the old bridge. Turn left, cross over the Loin Water and then turn left onto the access road to Stronafyne. Follow this to an obvious path on the right which leads to a path junction, signposted left to Inveruglas via Glen Loin. Turn right and follow the path which ascends steadily to a viewpoint overlooking Arrochar village.

Turn right at the next path junction and descend steeply to the main road and Arrochar. A right turn leads past the Loch Long Hotel back to the easterly car park and the walkway.

The old bridge at Arrochar

16 Glen Loin

From Arrochar to Coiregrogain

Ben Vane from Coriegrogain

This walk takes forest tracks and ancient paths to link Arrochar with Inveruglas on Loch Lomond, via Glen Loin and Coiregrogain, passing below some the highest hills in the area. The route is very straightforward and easily followed, but it is also very long and best saved for a settled mid-summer day when there will be no concerns about weather or limited daylight.

The walk can be started from either of the pay and display car parks at the head of Loch Long. From the most westerly of the car parks – they are linked by a walkway – gain the access path to **The Cobbler** [18] and zigzag up the hillside to the upper track.

Turn right and follow the track past a junction, **Succoth Loop** [15] heads off down right, to ascend steadily around the flanks of A' Chrois, with fine views back across Loch Long to a high point between the glens. **Ben Vorlich** [46] lies straight ahead with Ben Lomond poking its head up beside **Cruach Taibeirt** [13] to the east. The return path can also be seen beside the pylons in Glen Loin below.

The view opens up over Coiregrogain to the Loch Sloy dam between Ben Vorlich and **Ben Vane** [48] as the track traverses west through open conifer plantations to below the craggy north face of Beinn Ìme, with **Beinn Chorranach** [23] beyond. Cross the Allt Coiregrogain burn at the head of the glen by a ford and continue past a waterfall and weir on the southern flanks of Ben Vane where the track starts its long descent to the floor of the glen.

Cross the bridge below the dam onto the tarmac access road and follow it

START & FINISH: *Loch Long car parks on A83, Arrochar*

DISTANCE: *17.5km; 10.75 miles*

TIME: *5hrs*

MAP: *OS 56; Harvey LLTOA*

TERRAIN: *Tracks and paths; rough in places*

GRADE: *Moderate*

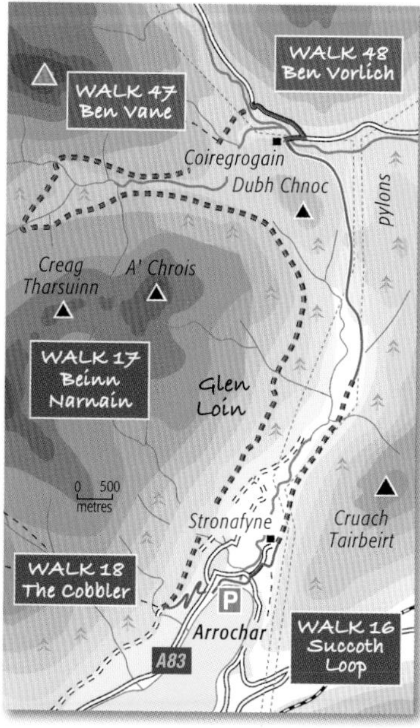

east to a marker post at the track junction signposted Arrochar via Glen Loin 8km (5 miles). Follow the track down towards Coiregrogain farm and over a bridge beyond which a path starts on the left at a kissing gate.

Follow the ascending path into forest and round to open ground and double lines of electricity pylons. Ascend steadily to high point at a pylon with views across Loch Long to Ben Lomond and back to Ben Vorlich. The descent path is steep and eroded in places, but generally good and leads down to a gate and the glen floor. A track starts just after a footbridge and leads through gates to enter fields before Stronafyne farm. Leave the track for a path on the left which skirts round the farm and a new house to a junction.

Turn right – straight ahead leads to Arrochar village – and gain the farm access road which is followed back to the main road and car parks.

Descending towards Coiregrogain

17 Beinn Narnain & A' Chrois

A less-frequented route on a popular hill

Beinn Narnain is an aircraft carrier of a hill, impressive for both its bulk, flat top and craggy prow! Although often combined with Beinn Ìme and The Cobbler – all three hills meet at the Bealach a' Mhaim – Narnain also offers an excellent independent round when combined with A' Chrois, its fine easterly outlier.

This takes the walker off the beaten path and away from the Munro-bagging crowds for a circuit above the cliffs of Creag Tharsuinn to the summit of A' Chrois and views over Loch Sloy and Loch Lomond. A' Chrois's rounded summit is deceptive as its south-east face comprises steep cliffs, popular with mountaineers in the 1890s, but out of favour with today's 'crag rats'. The name is said to originate from the distinctive cross formed by late season snow in the vertical central gully and on the horizontal terrace below the cliffs.

Below Spearhead Arête

START & FINISH: *Loch Long car parks on A83, Arrochar*

DISTANCE: *13.5km; 8.25 miles*

TIME: *5hrs 30mins*

MAP: *OS 56; Harvey LLTOA*

TERRAIN: *Paths and pathless hillside; rocky and boggy in places*

GRADE: *Strenuous*

A' Chrois and Ben Lomond

From the most westerly car park, at the head of Loch Long, cross the road to The Cobbler access path and zigzag up the hillside to the upper track and communications mast. Continue straight up the hillside from near the mast to emerge beside the upper section of the Allt a' Bhalachain, the Buttermilk Burn, and follow it to where it divides, just short of a small dam.

Turn right and contour east round the hillside for almost 1km (0.75 mile), to where the old path ascending from the Loch Long car park cuts straight across and directly up Narnain's south-east spur. Follow this path, eroded and wet in places with a few scrambly sections, to gain the rounded top of Cruach nam Miseag and views of Narnain's craggy prow – the Spearhead Arete.

At first it is hard to see where the path goes among the crags and boulders, but a route soon emerges, weaving up the hillside to gain a steep scrambly gully right of the Spearhead, from where the relatively flat top can be traversed to the summit cairn and trig point.

The descent north-east to the ridge above Coire Sugach is rocky and scattered with small crags, but not steep and the lower grassy ridge is soon reached and followed over Creag Tharsuinn and assorted other rocky tops to the summit of A' Chrois. From here descend south-west then south following the high ground of the broad ridge to the forest edge and a small dam on the Allt Sugach, where the continuation of the horizontal path can be gained and followed back to the base of Narnain's south-east spur. Descending the old path is more direct, but the going is very rocky and rough and retracing your steps to the Cobbler path may be preferable.

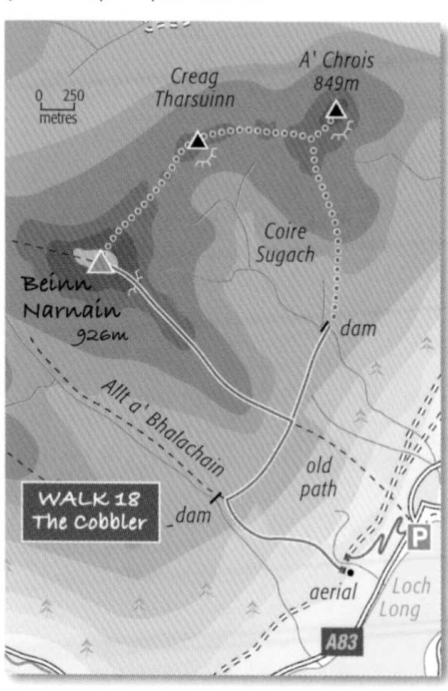

18 The Cobbler

Craggy centrepiece of the Arrochar Alps

South Peak with Ben Lomond beyond

There are few mountains in Scotland where the summit is only obtainable by rock climbing. True, the climb to the top of The Cobbler's Central Peak is very short, but it is a climb nonetheless and of all the people who ascend the mountain every day, only a handful can claim to have actually stood on the highest point.

Does it matter? No, of course not. In some ways the Central Peak is just a pimple on a ridge. Climb it if you wish, but don't loose sleep if you do not.

From the most westerly car park, at the head of Loch Long, cross the road to The Cobbler access path and zigzag up the hillside to the upper track and communications mast. Continue straight up the hillside from near the mast to emerge beside the upper section of the Allt a' Bhalachain, the Buttermilk Burn, and follow it to a small dam on the left.

Cross over the burn either above or below the dam depending on water flow and ascend the grassy hillside to gain the south-east ridge. This leads over various rocky bumps to the impressive South Peak. Skirt this on the left and ascend to the Centre Peak. This rocky pillar is the highest point of the mountain and involves a short but very exposed section of rock climbing to gain its summit. This is not for the nervous or the novice, and not recommended in wet or windy weather either.

Return to the path and contour round to the col below the North Peak, where the main path comes up from the right.

START & FINISH: *Loch Long car parks on A83, Arrochar*

DISTANCE: *10.5km; 6.5 miles*

TIME: *4hrs 30mins*

MAP: *OS 56; Harvey LLTOA*

TERRAIN: *Paths; muddy and rocky in places*

GRADE: *Strenuous*

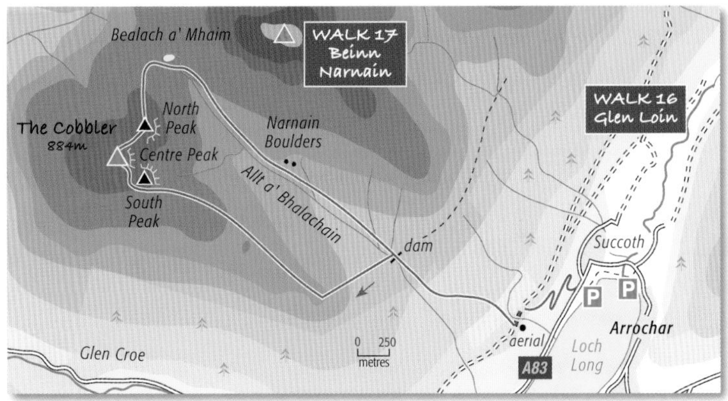

Despite the wildly overhanging nature of the peak's main rock face, getting to the summit only requires an easy scramble from the col.

Taking extra care, return to the path by the same route and contour round the north ridge of The Cobbler towards Bealach a' Mhaim. Parts of the path this quite steep but it soon arrives at the bealach, the broad saddle linking The Cobbler, Beinn Ìme and **Beinn Narnain** [17].

Turn south-east and descend the path beside the Allt a' Bhalachain. The main Cobbler path is soon joined and followed down past the massive Narnain Boulders to the dam and the path leading back to the car park.

South Peak, left, Centre Peak and North Peak

The Cobbler and Beinn Donich, left, from Loch Long

19 Cat Craig Loop

varied walking to the shores of Loch Long

Loch Long seashore

West of Arrochar, Ardgarten Visitor Centre at the foot of Glen Croe is the starting point for various walks among the surrounding woodland and hills overlooking Loch Long. The Cat Craig Loop started life as a cycle route, but is now more frequented by walkers, and can be combined with the riverside path near Ardgarten Campsite for the return journey. From the visitor centre car park (NN 269 037) go over the bridge, turn right and follow the forest track. This ascends steadily with views ahead to The Brack and **Ben Donich** [21] and back across Glen Croe to **The Cobbler** [18].

After some distance you join a higher track and turn left, following the Cat Craig Loop sign, to arrive at a picnic table with views down Glen Croe.

The route now starts to descend with some fleeting views to arrive at a low point where the track ends and a path begins. Ascend again and cross a footbridge before coming round to an unexpected view over Loch Long and the surrounding mountains. A steady descent leads to a flight of steps, a second picnic table and a viewpoint.

From there the track leads off into more forest and descends steadily to

Ardgarten Visitor Centre

START & FINISH: *Ardgarten Visitor Centre car park on A83*

DISTANCE: *9.5km; 6 miles*

TIME: *2hrs 30mins*

MAP: *OS 56; Harvey LLTOA*

TERRAIN: *Waymarked roads, tracks and paths*

GRADE: *Easy*

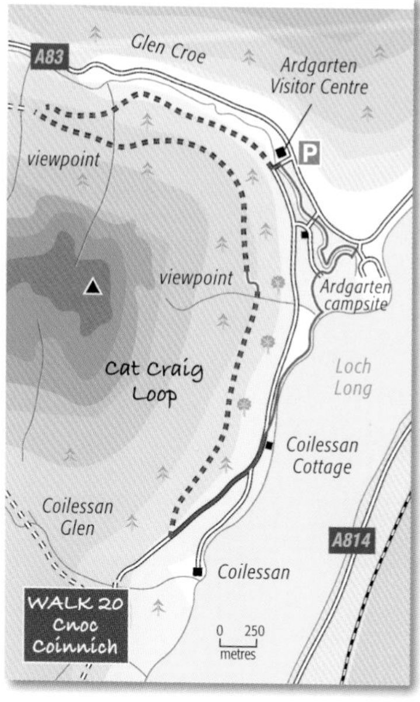

the tarmac access road. Turn left and follow the access road past the entry to Coilessan House and on past Coilessan Cottage. The road is a dead end and has little traffic, and is also part of the cycle route round the Ardgoil peninsula, but keep an ear out for vehicles nonetheless.

Just after Coilessan Cottage a waymarked route leaves the road and heads right into woodland to skirt a campsite and gain the loch shore. Follow the beach round, to where the waymarks lead inland through open woodland to gain an access road.

Turn right following waymarks to a sign indicating a footpath and follow this beside the river to cross a large footbridge and ascend to the Ardgarten Campsite access road. Turn immediately left following the sign to Ardgarten Visitor Centre and follow the path, now on the opposite bank of the river, through fine broadleaf woodland to the visitor centre car park.

Loch Long from the second viewpoint

20 Cnoc Coinnich

Off the beaten path on a hidden gem

Ben Donich, left, and Cnoc Coinnich from the south

Situated at the head of the Ardgoil peninsula between Loch Long and Loch Goil, Cnoc Coinnich offers some of the best views in the Arrochar area.

Obscured from many directions by its higher and bigger neighbours The Brack and **Ben Donich** [21] and overshadowed by the scene-stealing grandeur of **The Cobbler** [18], Cnoc Coinnich's summit is relatively unfrequented. However, ease of access from Ardgarten Visitor Centre and a relatively straightforward ascent combined with spectacular views and no crowds make Cnoc Coinnich a hidden gem for anyone willing to step off the beaten track.

From Ardgarten Visitor Centre at the foot of Glen Croe drive over the bridge, turn left and follow the access road to where it ends at the large Coilessan Events car park below the Coilessan Glen (NN 258 011). Care should be taken on this narrow road which is mostly used by walkers and cyclists.

Cnoc Coinnich summit

Continue on the track through the locked gate and cross the bridge over the burn. Shortly after this turn right where the track divides, following the Coilessan Glen Road signpost. The track ascends steadily through conifers

START & FINISH: *Coilessan Glen Events car park, off A83*

DISTANCE: *9.5km; 6 miles*

TIME: *3hrs 15mins*

MAP: *OS 56; Harvey LLTOA*

TERRAIN: *Tracks, paths and pathless hillside; boggy in places*

GRADE: *Moderate*

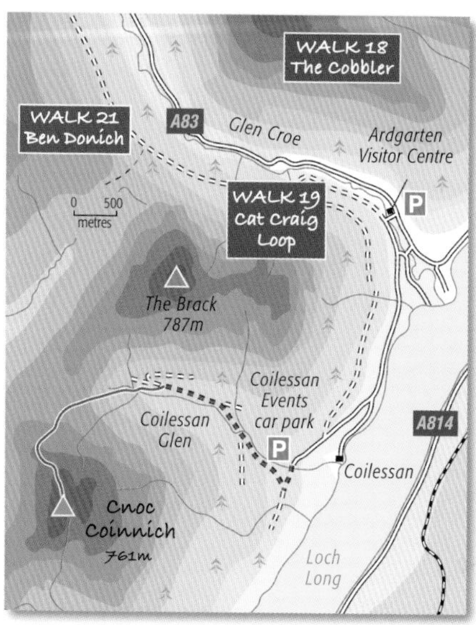

with views to the craggy southern flanks of The Brack.

Remain on the track at the next fork where the cycle route goes off left, go over a bridge and follow the track up the glen with increasing views left to Cnoc Coinnich. Keep straight ahead at the next track junction and follow the track to where another track goes off to the right. Just down left from this is a turning area with a footpath signposted Lochgoilhead 6km (3.75 miles).

Cross two footbridges then ascend beside the burn through the forest to gain the open hillside. Follow the footpath, indistinct in places, then head off left picking the least boggy route to gain the north ridge of Cnoc Coinnich, which leads quickly to the summit marked by a cairn on the edge of a small cliff. After admiring the classic West Coast view of mountains and sea lochs, return by the same route.

Ascending to the north ridge; The Brack in the background

21 Ben Donich

A fine mountain with the best left until last!

Beinn an Lochain, left, and Loch Restil

Ben Donich rises above the 'Rest and be thankful', the aptly named high point between glens Croe and Kinglas. While it isn't quite as dramatic an ascent as **Beinn an Lochain** [22], immediately to the north, the summit commands superb views over the Clyde sea lochs.

For most walkers the north ridge is the line of ascent and descent, but the route described here traverses forest tracks round into Glen Croe to ascend the broader and pathless south-east ridge, leaving the spectacular views from the steep north ridge to be savoured in descent.

Start directly below the mountain at the Forestry Commission car park on the Lochgoilhead road (NN 227 069), just beyond the 'Rest and be thankful', Follow the track to a turning on the left by an aerial, go round the gate and descend the track into Glen Croe. Fork right where the track divides and rise steadily through the forest, passing a viewpoint and picnic area with benches, to arrive, after about 30 minutes, at an obvious path leading off right into forest. This is marked with a white post and is signposted to Lochgoilhead and Ardgarten.

This path ascends steeply through the forest then levels out to a stile in the perimeter fence and open hillside. Continue south-west then gain the open south-east face, with fine views back to The Brack, **Ben Reoch** [12] above Loch Long and distant Ben Lomond. Across Glen Croe the pointed North Peak of **The Cobbler** [18] is prominent, then Beinn Ìme and Beinn Luibhean with **Beinn an Lochain** [22] beyond.

As height is gained the south-east ridge becomes better defined and leads to a well-worn path across the

START & FINISH: *Forestry car park on the B828*

DISTANCE: *9.5km; 6 miles*

TIME: *3hrs 30mins*

MAP: *OS 56; Harvey LLTOA*

TERRAIN: *Tracks, paths and pathless hillside; boggy in places*

GRADE: *Moderate / Strenuous*

broad summit plateau, which is followed west to the trig point. To the south and west Arran and the lochs and islands of the Clyde now dominate the view and, when the visibility is good, the Paps of Jura can be seen beyond Cowal and Kintyre.

For the descent follow the clear path down the north ridge to where the west facing cliffs of Coire Culach abut the ridge. With a little bit of scrambling, the path weaves between massive boulders and crevasses in the mica schist rock. On a fine day this is no problem, but extra care should be taken in poor visibility or in the wet as some of the holes are deep and wide, and the worn rock slippery when wet. Beyond this point increasingly spectacular views open out to Beinn an Lochain towering over Loch Restil and the 'Rest and be thankful'.

Continue descending to a stile into felled forestry and a footpath leading to the forest track. Turn right and follow the track back to the car park.

The Cobbler and distant Ben Lomond from the south-east ridge

22 Beinn an Lochain

Classic peak of the Arrochar Alps

Beinn an Lochain from Glen Croe

Beinn an Lochain's north-east ridge offers a classic ascent with a distinctly mountaineering atmosphere and superb situations, high above Glen Kinglas and Glen Croe.

The ridge is surprisingly narrow and rocky with a few scrambly sections, but nothing too exposed nor too serious. Nevertheless, it is not a route for the inexperienced hillwalker and should be avoided in bad weather and especially so when it is windy.

The best starting point is a large layby on the west side of the A83, just beyond Loch Restil, as the road starts to descend to Glen Kinglas (NN 232 086). Cross over the burn flowing from the loch and follow a path, a little ill-defined at first, which aims for and then gains the north-east ridge. Once on the ridge the path is obvious and height is quickly gained, assisted in part by the fact that the path joins the ridge some way above the floor of the glen. Beinn an Lochain is made of mica schist rock, but the ridge is scattered with large granite boulders ripped from distant peaks and deposited by a

START & FINISH: *Butterbridge car park on the A83, Glen Kinglas*

DISTANCE: *5km; 3 miles*

TIME: *2 hrs 30mins*

MAP: *OS 56; Harvey LLTOA*

TERRAIN: *Paths; boggy and rocky in places*

GRADE: *Moderate / Strenuous*

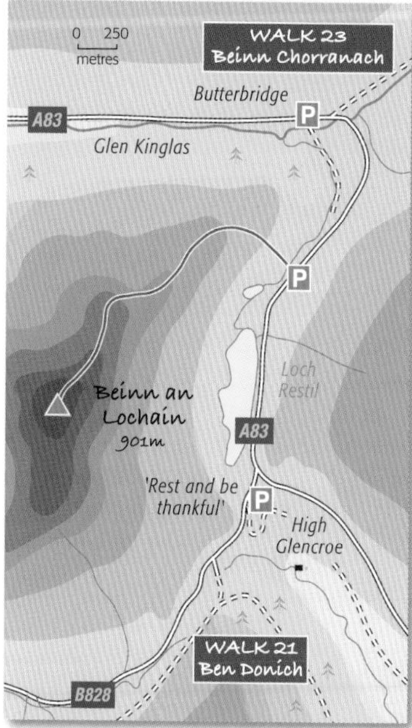

passing glacier. Similar 'glacial erratics' can be found below **The Cobbler** [18].

The ridge is followed to the first line of cliffs which are skirted via a diagonal left to right path above them. Care should be taken here especially in descent, or when the ground is wet, as the cliffs lie directly below. The path then regains the ridge forming the south wall of the large north corrie.

Avoid the final steep section of the ridge on the left and ascend steeply to the top of the ridge and the summit cairn a short distance beyond. The view from the summit area is particularly good ranging from Loch Goil, Loch Long and the Clyde in the south to Ben More, Stob Binnein and the Crianlarich hills to the north-east.

From the summit the best descent is via the line of ascent, but it is also possible to continue to the south summit and descend the steep east face to the B828 at the 'Rest and be thankful' and follow the very busy A83 alongside Loch Restil back to the layby.

Left and above, Beinn an Lochain from upper Glen Kinglas

23 Beinn Chorranach

An unjustly neglected mountain

Beinn Chorranach, left, and Beinn Ìme from Butterbridge

The Beinn Ìme massif comprises three principal hills: Beinn Ìme, Beinn Chorranach and Beinn Luibhean. Ìme is one of the popular Arrochar Munros and gets plenty of visitors, as does the Corbett Beinn Luibhean, but the other hill in this triumvirate, Beinn Chorranach, hardly sees a soul. Despite being higher than Luibhean there is insufficient height difference between Chorranach and Ìme to put Chorranach on the Corbett tick list. Visitors are likely to have the hill to themselves and there are no wide paths, but the ascent requires a bit of route finding as a consequence.

Beinn Chorranach's north ridge gives the finest ascent and an optional extension can be made to Beinn Ìme for any Munro baggers in the party. From the car park at Butterbridge in Glen Kinglas (NN 234 095), follow the track north-west through the upper Kinglas glen, to the red-roofed cottage of Abyssinia. Leave the main track, ford the Kinglas Water by stepping stones and ascend the track to the old cottage.

Skirt the building on the right to gain a small burn and follow its left bank straight up the hillside to a deer fence. Do not cross over, but follow good animal tracks below it for a few minutes, east and then south into Gleann Uaine, to a ladder stile. Cross over and ascend the hillside to the north ridge of Beinn Chorranach, with steadily improving views east to **Ben Vane** [48], Loch Lomond and Ben Ledi, and south to craggy **A' Chrois** [17], the cliffs of Beinn Ìme and Ben Lomond.

Follow the long ridge to the summit cairn and views north to Beinn Bhuidhe, Ben Cruachan and the Ben

START & FINISH: *Butterbridge car park on the A83, Glen Kinglas*

DISTANCE: *9.5km; 6 miles*

TIME: *3hrs 45mins*

MAP: *OS 56; Harvey LLTOA*

TERRAIN: *Tracks, paths and pathless hillside; rough and rocky in places*

GRADE: *Strenuous*

0 500
metres
Abyssinia
deer fence
stile
Glen Kinglas
Stob Coire Creagach
Butterbridge
P
Beinn Chorranach
885m
aerial
Glas Bhealach
Beinn Ìme
1011m
Beinn Luibhean
Loch Restil
High Glencroe
Bealach a' Mhaim

Lui group. Descend to Glas Bhealach, the col below Beinn Ìme, and a choice of routes; directly west into the glen, or up Beinn Ìme. To descend, follow the slopes into the glen to gain the west side of the burn, where a rough path leads beside felled forestry to an aerial on a small hillock on the left. Cross a fence to gain the aerial, from where a track leads down to the road. Go straight over and pick the driest line to gain the partially overgrown old tarmac road in the floor of the glen. Follow it back over General Wade's 'Butterbridge' to the car park.

If continuing over Beinn Ìme from Beinn Chorranach, take the path that appears above the col and follow it easily to the summit. From there continue south on a path heading for The Cobbler and Bealach a' Mhaim, until it can be left for a gradual descent to the col between Ìme and Beinn Luibhean. From the col, follow the right (east) side of the burn draining north and descend into the small glen below Ìme's west face and the Glas Bhealach. Beyond the old sheep pens where the glen levels out, gain the path on the burn's west side (add 2.5km and 1hr).

Beinn Chorranach and the Glas Bhealach from Beinn Ìme

Lochgoilhead

The Brack, left, and Cnoc Coinnich above Lochgoilhead

Surrounded on all sides by high mountains and accessible only by boat, or single track road from the north or west, Lochgoilhead feels more remote than all of the other areas in this guidebook. In reality this is not the case and the village is only a short drive west from Arrochar, Tarbet and Loch Lomond.

Lochgoilhead and nearby Drimsynie have a number of holiday homes and chalets, with water sports and golf being the recreational choice for most visitors. The area also offers some excellent walking and while the surrounding hills are not the highest, they combine a distinct character with a level of solitude that is almost impossible among the 'Arrochar Alps' further north.

The largest hill in the area, **Beinn Bheula** [32], faces Lochgoilhead across Loch Goil and while it can be climbed from the village via the Curra Lochain, an ascent from Loch Eck has been chosen in preference and is described in the Cowal chapter. In some respects the smaller Stob na Boine Druim-fhinn [26] to the north, is a more consistently interesting mountain and is easily accessed from Lochgoilhead. The other hillwalk in this chapter is Cruach nam Miseag [27] above Lochain nan

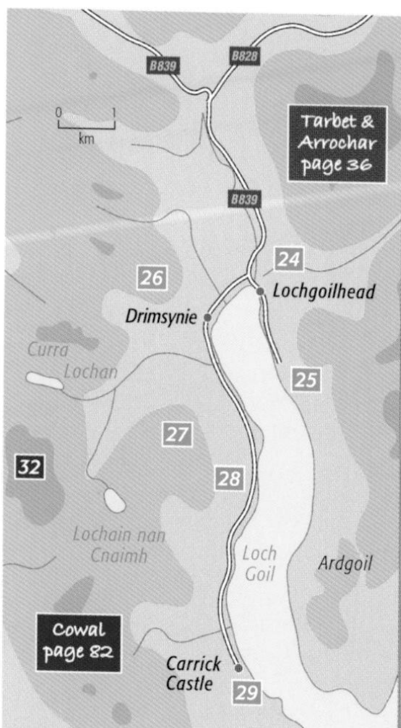

Cnaimh. This small easterly outlier of Beinn Bheula overlooks Loch Goil and is best viewed from Carrick Castle to the south, where it presents an impressively pointed profile out of proportion to its modest height, (see p76 and 80).

The remaining four walks in this chapter stick to the lower ground. Glen Donich [24] between **Ben Donich** [21] and **Cnoc Coinnich** [20], with its woodland and waterfalls, offers fine views over the village and Loch Goil. The route round the shore of East Loch Goil [25] is significantly longer and utilises forest tracks and the cycle route round the Ardgoil peninsula.

Cormonochan Woodland [28] on the west side of Loch Goil combines a section of the old road to Carrick Castle with a specially created trail through sections of ancient broadleaf woodland above the loch. Red squirrels are a feature of this walk and the route is enhanced by wooden sculptures and information boards created with the assistance of local schoolchildren.

If Lochgoilhead feels remote then Carrick Castle further south down Loch Goil feels doubly so. However, a large car park at the castle allows easy access to the shore of Loch Goil and the surrounding hills.

South from Carrick Castle [29] follows the traditional route to Glen Finart and Ardentinny (see Cowal p82). This route is a longish walk utilising shoreline, paths and forest tracks and can be combined with a number of walks in the Cowal chapter including a high level return to Carrick Castle via Am Binnein, Creachan Mòr and Cruach an Draghair.

GETTING THERE

Road: *From Glasgow & Edinburgh – M8, A82, A83, B828, B839. From Stirling – A811, A82, then as Glasgow*

Bus: *See pages 10 & 11*

TOWNS & VILLAGES

Lochgoilhead: *Shops, hotels, restaurant, cafe*

ACCOMMODATION

Lochgoilhead and Drymsynie have a few hotels and a range of bed and breakfast. Bed and breakfast can also be found at Carrick Castle. See also pages 10 & 11

24 Glen Donich

Relaxing forest walking with fine views

Descending to Lochgoilhead

Surrounded by high hills, Lochgoilhead offers classic western seaboard scenery and although this is quite a short walk, it gives a good introduction to the area.

Start from the Argyll Forest Park, Lochgoilhead Arboretum car park opposite the fire station and primary school in Hall Road (NN 200 016). This is the road leading from the drinking fountain near the lochside car park.

Follow the path into the conifer woodland, turning left, right, then left again to where steps lead up to a forestry track. Turn right and follow the track to a gate where a path ascends on the left to a wooden gate and an upper track. You are now on the Cowal Way, the 75km (47 mile) walkers' route from Portavadie at the south-west end of the Cowal peninsula to Ardgarten on Loch Long.

Initially the track ascends quite steeply with an increasingly good view of Loch Goil and the surrounding hills, then levels out as you pass through an area of younger trees. Noise of the Donich Water in the glen below starts to increase and you descend to the waterfalls and rapids that mark the halfway point in the walk.

Cross a footbridge – a sign indicates a path off left to Donich Glen and Coilessan Hill Path – and traverse the forest hillside above the waterfalls. With great care it is possible to scramble down to the base of the falls. Continue on over a second bridge and rise up to a picnic table with a fine view down the glen and across Loch Goil to **Beinn Bheula** [32], the highest

START & FINISH: *Lochgoilhead Arboretum car park, Hall Road*

DISTANCE: *4km; 2.5 miles*

TIME: *1hr 15mins*

MAP: *OS 56; Harvey LLTOA*

TERRAIN: *Waymarked tracks and paths*

GRADE: *Easy*

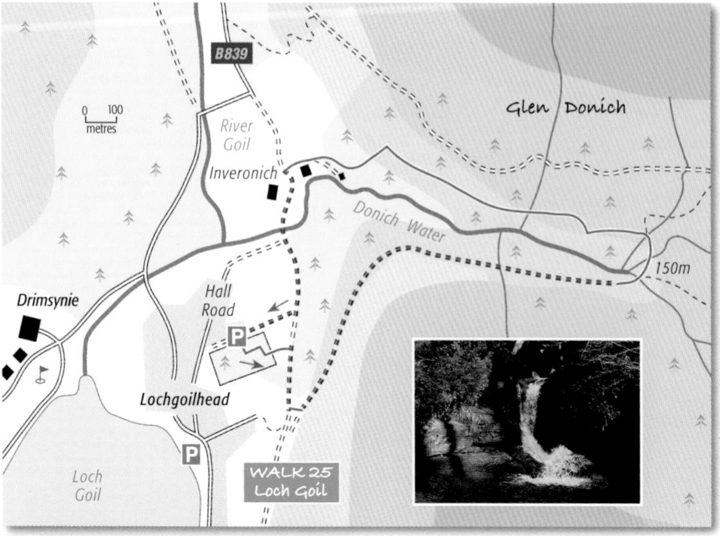

B839
0 100 metres
River Goil
Inveronich
Glen Donich
Donich Water
150m
Drimsynie
Hall Road
Lochgoilhead
Loch Goil
WALK 25 Loch Goil

West to the mountains

hill in the area, with Beinn Lochain, Beinn Tharsuinn and Stob na Boine Druim-fhinn [26] to its right. Continue ascending to a path junction where a sign indicates the new Lochgoilhead to Glen Croe path rising steeply through the trees. Don't follow this route, but continue round on the path as it starts its descent back to Lochgoilhead.

The path continues round and levels out to give a fantastic panorama of the surrounding hills through the conifers and down to the village and Drimsynie. Descend quite steeply through the forest to arrive at a track and follow it down through the farmyard of Inveronich to join the access track from the main road.

Turn left onto the track and follow it through a gate with a stile then over the Donich Water, beyond which the next right leads back to the car park.

25 East Loch Goil

Exploring the Ardgoil peninsula

Lochgoilhead

South of Lochgoilhead, a mountain biking trail can be followed round the tip of the Ardgoil peninsula and north up Loch Long to Ardgarten, from where it continues north up Glen Croe, round Ben Donich and back south to Lochgoilhead. Like many of the walks in this area, this route utilises part of the cycle trail to create an enjoyable circular outing above the east shore of Loch Goil. The bike trail is on wide, but rough gravel tracks and while there is room for all, walkers should keep an ear out for fast-approaching bikers.

Park at the large car park on the lochside in the centre of Lochgoilhead and follow the private road south along the east shore of Loch Goil. After about 1km (0.75 mile) leave the road at a

Ruined sheep pens above Loch Goil

START & FINISH: *Lochgoilhead main lochside car park*

DISTANCE: *9.5km; 6 miles*

TIME: *2hrs 45mins*

MAP: *OS 56, 63; Harvey LLTOA*

TERRAIN: *Signposted roads, tracks and paths; steep in places*

GRADE: *Easy / moderate*

wooden barrier and follow an obvious path up through conifer woodland to a track. A signpost on the other side indicates the cycle route to Duke's Pass and Corran Lochan: the return route.

Descend rightwards on the track which undulates along the east side of the loch, passing a fine waterfall and an open area with views across the loch to Carrick and Lochgoilhead. A steady descent then follows to just before the burn draining into Loch Goil at Stuckbeg. Here a path leaves the track off to the left, opposite a sign pointing back to Lochgoilhead, and ascends steeply to meet the upper cycle track between two gates.

Turn left back to Lochgoilhead (the right turn leads through forest to open hillside, a high point, and a descent to Corran Lochan) and follow the path down through conifer and broadleaf forest. Cross a footbridge into a felled area passing ruins and old sheep pens

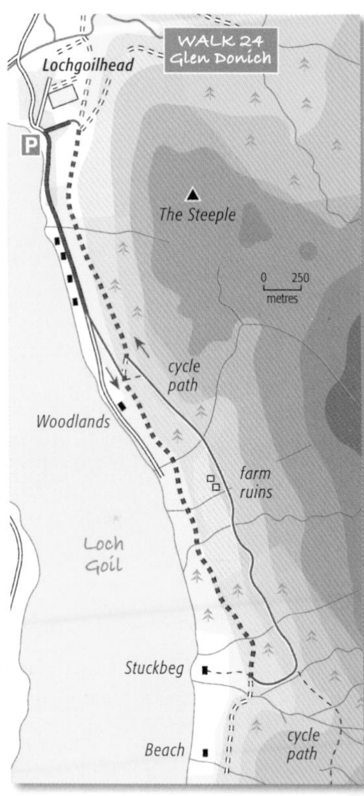

and on over another bridge into conifers, from where a final steep descent regains the track.

Turn right, signposted Lochgoilhead 2km (1.25 miles), and follow the track to a gate, stile and bench, with fine views north to the mountains above Lochgoilhead and Drimsynie House. Just before the track divides, a path leads off left at an electricity pole to a gate and stile and a descent between houses back to the main road and car park.

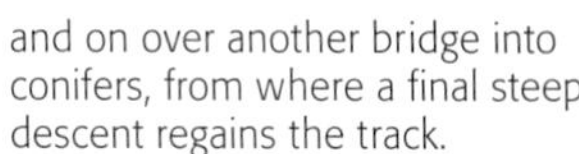

26 Stob na Boine Druim-fhinn

An unexpectedly rocky and characterful hill

Approaching the summit

What's in a name? Stob na Boine Druim-fhinn is the longest mountain name in this book, but it's a name which appeared on the maps comparatively recently. The 1949 edition of the Scottish Mountaineering Club's definitive guide to the *Southern Highlands* notes the peak as unnamed. By the 1972 edition the name had appeared.

Perhaps the trig point was added between the two dates, necessitating the need for a name? If so, was it a local name, or did someone make it up? The latter is not so fanciful as it might sound. The Scottish Mountaineering Club has named a few hills in the course of defining its lists of Munro and Corbett summits.

Whatever the origins of the name, it's a hill of character, a broad airy ridge with a rocky step leading to a surprisingly rocky summit.

There is limited parking on Loch Goil south of the Drimsynie chalets (NN 189 005). Continue up the road and turn right to Drimsynie Estate Office (Corrow Farm) and a walking route round 'Glen Ban'. Go through the farmyard and follow the track beyond as it bends right and ascends to a track junction below an obvious firebreak.

Ascend a well-worn sheep path up the firebreak past an aerial and through a gate to an upper gate on a new forestry track. Cross straight over and continue ascending to exit the forest below a small craggy bluff. The sheep path continues beside the forest, but the bluff can be skirted on the right or left to gain the broad ridge above and views south to Beinn Lochain and the

START & FINISH: *Off road parking on Loch Goil*

DISTANCE: *8km; 5 miles*

TIME: *3hrs*

MAP: *OS 56; Harvey LLTOA*

TERRAIN: *Tracks, paths and pathless hillside*

GRADE: *Moderate / Strenuous*

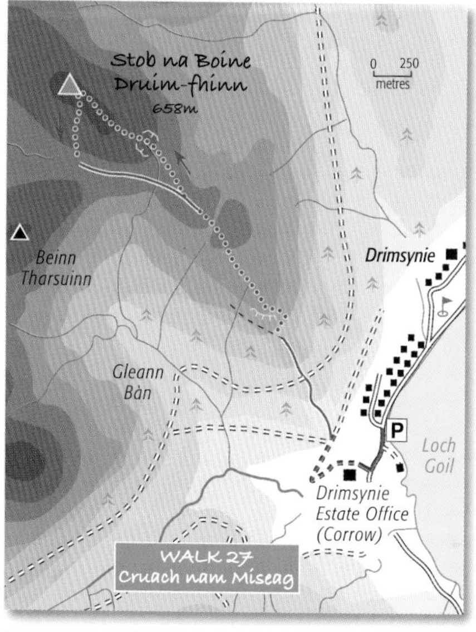

Caisteal Dubh, the Black Castle cliffs of **Beinn Bheula** [32].

Follow the broad ridge aiming for the obvious deep cleft (NS 17431 02157) in the terraced cliffs straight ahead. Ascend the cleft beside the burn to regain the broad ridge and a final section of narrower ridge leading to the summit rocks and trig point.

A pleasant return route can be had via the col between Stob na Boine Druim-fhinn and Creag Tharsuinn to the south. Descend from the summit rocks to the broader ridge then descend south to the col at the head of the Coirein Rathaid. From here traverse east below the terraced cliffs and cleft to gain the initial broad ridge and retrace your steps to the start.

The cleft in the cliffs

27 Cruach nam Miseag

An impressive small peak with fine views

Cruach nam Miseag from Drimsynie

Viewed from Carrick Castle to the south, (see p76, 77, 80), Cruach nam Miseag presents a striking profile for a peak of such modest height. Across Loch Goil from the north the profile is less dramatic, but the hill still holds its own among the much higher hills which surround it.

Limited parking can be had on Loch Goil south of the Drimsynie chalets (NN 189 005). Continue up the road past Drimsynie Estate Office (Corrow Farm) and over the Lettermay Burn to the next right turning to Lettermay. Follow the track up left to a house, then right into Forestry Commission Scotland woodland on the northern flanks of Cruach nam Miseag.

Continue on the track to a point where a right-hand bend turns back left into the glen and the mountain Beinn Lochain is framed straight ahead above the forest. At this point keep an eye out for a small track on the left heading into the forest; NN 17958 00034 and about 1km (0.75 mile) from the upper house. The track is shown in the Harvey *Loch Lomond & The Trossachs Outdoor Atlas*, but not on Ordnance Survey maps.

The track exits from the forest and starts zigzagging up the open hillside, offering excellent views across Lochgoilhead. Follow it to where it fades, then head right to gain and follow a stream bed passing over various false and craggy summits to the two prominent final tops. The highest is the left-hand one, guarded to north and east by impressive cliffs. Gain its broad north ridge and follow it to the small cairn marking the summit with its impressive landscape of sea and mountains in all directions.

From the summit go west towards **Beinn Bheula** [32] to the final small top overlooking Lochain nan Cnaimh, before returning towards Cruach nam Miseag to pick up the ascent route and reverse it to Lochgoilhead.

START & FINISH: *Off road parking on Loch Goil*

DISTANCE: *10.5km; 6.5 miles*

TIME: *3hrs 30mins*

MAP: *OS 56; Harvey LLTOA*

TERRAIN: *Tracks, paths and pathless hillside; boggy in places*

GRADE: *Moderate / Strenuous*

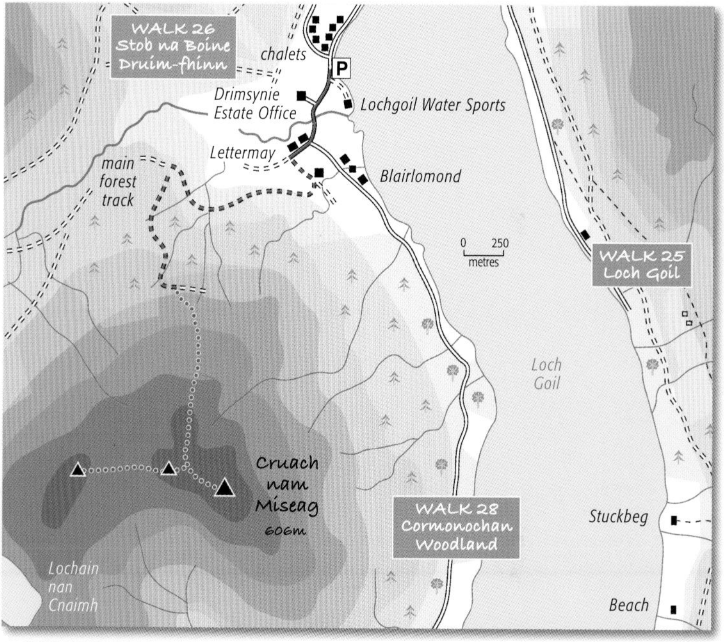

Cruach nam Miseag and Lochain nan Cnaimh from Beinn Bheula

Cruach nam Miseag
from the foot of Loch Goil

28 Cormonachan Woodland

Red squirrels on the old road to Carrick Castle

Jan's Hideaway above Loch Goil

Although short, this walk explores a beautiful part of the mature woodland on the western shores of Loch Goil, utilising the old road to Carrick Castle and offering fine views to the hills of the Ardgoil peninsula.

The route follows the specially-created Red Squirrel Trail through Cormonachan Community Woodland and is well suited to youngsters, with interpretation boards describing the fauna and flora to be seen en route and squirrels carved from posts and tree stumps along the way.

Limited parking is possible beside the aerial, marked on OS and Harvey maps (NS 196 976), or in the large layby near the top of the hill. From the back of the fenced compound surrounding the aerial, follow the Red Squirrel Trail

START & FINISH: *Parking at aerial on the Carrick Castle road*

DISTANCE: *3km; 1.75 miles*

TIME: *45mins*

MAP: *OS 56; Harvey LLTOA*

TERRAIN: *Waymarked paths with interpretation boards*

GRADE: *Easy*

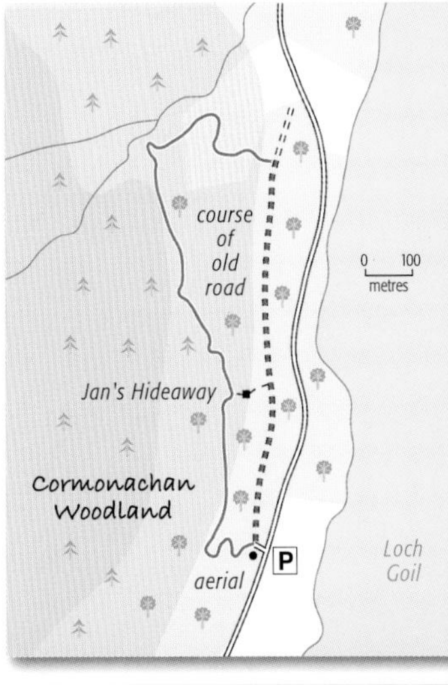

signs left and ascend to a bench and a viewpoint over Loch Goil. The path then levels out through broadleaf woodland of silver birch, beech, oak and occasional conifers, with further views right down to the loch and the hills beyond.

Turn left at the three-way junction. A sign points down right to a picnic bench and the roof of Jan's Hideaway, a wooden hut used as a field centre by local schools and outdoor centres.

Keep left and ascend into conifer woodland, then zigzag down through felled areas to join the line of the old road ascending from the loch shore. From here a steady ascent leads up through beautiful mature broadleaf woodland back to the starting point, passing a path leading right to Jan's Hideaway.

Old road to Carrick Castle

29 South from Carrick Castle

Finart Bay via Loch Goil and Loch Long

Cruach nam Miseag and Carrick Castle

This walk follows an old route along the shores of Loch Goil and Loch Long, from Carrick Castle to Glen Finart. The route is not technically demanding or particularly strenuous, but it is long and while there are waymarks here and there, care is needed to remain on the correct route. Two sections are quite boggy, but they can be bypassed with care.

From the car park at Carrick Castle, follow the road south until the houses end and it becomes a track leading to Ardnahein farm. Immediately before the gate into the farmyard a white stile on the right, signposted Ardentinny, gives access to a path skirting the farm to the south. The path can be very muddy in places, although the worst can be avoided.

Follow the fence to a stile and continue descending towards the shoreline. A faint inland path can be followed from here, but it is very rocky and boggy, and best avoided. Descend left to the shore and, depending a little on the state of the tide, traverse the rocky shoreline with care, round to the shingle headland before Toll nam Muc. Walk round the shingle headland, or straight across the meadow to beyond the head of the next bay where a white marker post on the right (NN 20412 93199) indicates a convenient rock by the fence, which allows you to step over it into woodland. From here a well-defined path ascends through bracken into broadleaf woodland with fine views back to Lochgoilhead and across to Ardgoil and Loch Long.

START & FINISH: *Carrick Castle car park*

DISTANCE: *17.5km; 10.75 miles*

TIME: *5hrs*

MAP: *OS 56; Harvey LLTOA*

TERRAIN: *Roads, tracks and waymarked paths; boggy in places*

GRADE: *Moderate / Strenuous*

Cross a stile and Carrick Castle footbridge, built in 1998 by the Officer Training Corps of Queen's University in Northern Ireland, and continue ascending through birch and oak to enter conifer forest and join a wide prepared path. Newly felled forestry leads to a forest track and waymark. Turn left and descend the track in long curves towards the loch shore, passing below electricity pylons.

More broadleaf woodland appears on the loch shore and the Naval base at Coulport comes into view across Loch Long. Continue past the ruin at **Knap Burn** [36] with views up right to the rocky top of **Am Binnein** [35] on the ridge above. Remain on the shore track until it rises to a junction and keep left, to descend past a gate to the sandy beach of Finart Bay and Ardentinny.

Return by the outward route or over the hills to Carrick Castle via Am Binnein, Creachan Mòr and Cruach an Draghair (see description on p94). The time and distance for this hill route is slightly more than returning by way of lochs Long and Goil and the added height gain shifts the whole route into the Strenuous category.

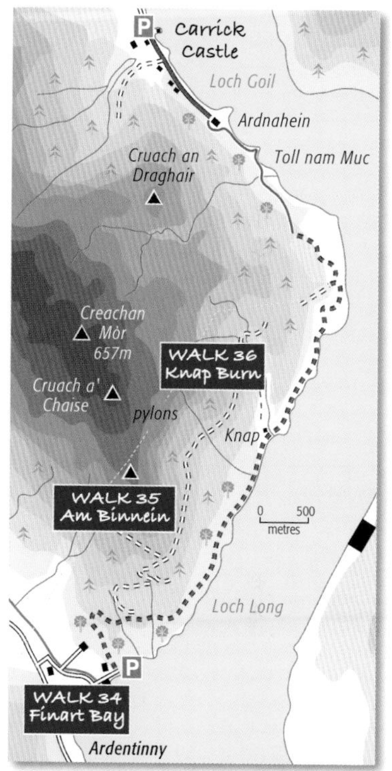

Paddle steamer SS Waverley entering Loch Goil

Cowal

Am Binnein from Ardentinny

Firmly rooted in the Highlands, but easily reached from Glasgow and the Clyde, the Cowal peninsula offers a wide range of opportunities for walkers of all abilities.

Only the high hills surrounding Loch Eck and the Clyde coastline north of Dunoon lie within the National Park boundary, but included within this area is land and lochscape comparable with any of the better known areas.

The jewel in the crown is the spectacular Royal Botanic Garden at **Benmore** [40]. The garden contains a large collection of trees and shrubs suited to the Clyde's warm and moist, Gulf Stream fed climate, including a grove of giant sequoia redwoods. **Benmore to Uig** [42] also features redwoods and other exotic trees, as does the walk around **Kilmun Arboretum** [44].

Before road became king, access was exclusively by boat across the 5km (3 miles) of the Clyde separating Dunoon from Gourock. Regular vehicle and passenger ferries continue to ply this route making it an enjoyable and relaxing method of visiting the area.

In the late 19th and early 20th centuries, relative isolation combined with easy boat access nurtured country estates at **Glenbranter** [30], one time home of music hall legend Sir Harry Lauder, Glen Finart and Benmore, and attracted day trippers and holiday makers from the Clyde cities. The delightful 'romantic' gorge of **Puck's Glen** [43] with its narrow paths and stone steps cut into the hillside dates from this time.

In the 1950s widespread conifer plantations started to cover the lower mountain slopes. Old paths were lost and new tracks hidden in dense forest. In the past decade, the steady opening of Forestry Commission Scotland

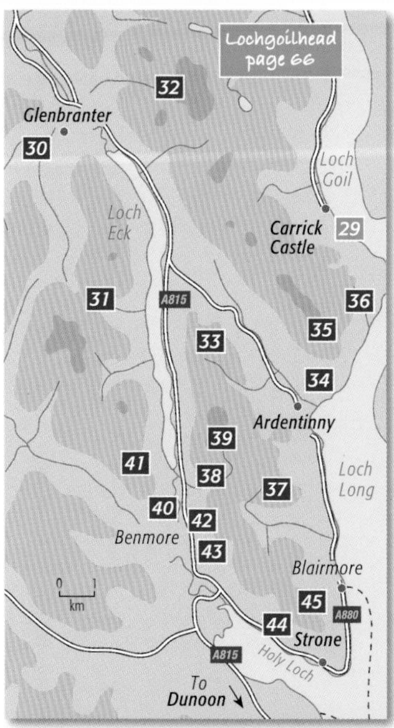

woodland to public access and the associated development of walking routes and cycle tracks, combined with more detailed Ordnance Survey maps, has encouraged walkers back to the area and Cowal now also supports an arts and walking festival – Cowalfest <www.cowalfest.org>.

At 779m **Beinn Bheula** [32] is the highest hill in the area. To the south, **Beinn Ruadh** [39], and the smaller **Sligrachan Hill** [33] offer shorter walks to viewpoints over Loch Eck and Loch Long. The remaining hills in this chapter – **A' Chruach** [41] above Benmore, **Am Binnein** [35] and **Stronchullin Hill** [37] near Ardentinny and **Strone Hill** [45] above Strone – are all small hills, even for Cowal, but they offer spectacular views over the Firth of Clyde and its associated sea lochs.

For coastal walkers, the sandy beach at **Finart Bay** [34] should not be missed, while the route beside Loch Long to **Knap** [36] offers a perspective on Cowal's agricultural past and naval present.

GETTING THERE

Road: *From Glasgow & Edinburgh – M8, A82, A83, A815. From Stirling – A811, A82, then as Glasgow*

Bus: *See pages 10 & 11*

Clyde Ferry: *Gourock – Dunoon (car) <www.calmac.co.uk>*
McInroy's Point (Gourock) – Hunter's Quay (Dunoon) (car) <www.western-ferries.co.uk>
Greenock – Blairmore (foot) <www.secondsnark.co.uk>

TOWNS & VILLAGES

Glenbranter: *Public toilets*

Ardentinny: *Bars, public toilets*

Benmore: *Cafe, toilets*

Blairmore / Strone: *Shop*

Orchard: *Shop, petrol station*

Dunoon *(south of National Park): All facilities inc bicycle hire*

TOURIST INFORMATION CENTRES (TIC)

Dunoon: *Alexandra Parade (08707 200 629)*

ACCOMMODATION

Centred on Dunoon (south of National Park boundary), but scattered hotels and bed and breakfast can be found throughout the area. Campsites at Inverchapel, Invereck, Orchard

30 Glenbranter

One time home of the great Sir Harry Lauder

The lower Allt Robuic

Glenbranter lies at the head of Loch Eck and was once the home of music hall legend Sir Harry Lauder. After his son John was killed in World War One, Lauder left Glenbranter never to return and his house is no longer standing. There are memorials to John Lauder and his mother Ann Vallance at Invernoaden, near the start of the route up **Beinn Bheula** [32].

Today, Glenbranter houses Forestry Commission Scotland, extensive conifer plantations and a number of way-marked trails. The highlight of this walk is the fine waterfalls in the steep glen of the Allt Robuic burn.

From the far end of the main car park (NS 110 978), continue straight ahead following a path with red, blue and yellow waymarks. Where the path forks keep left, the return route comes in

Upper falls, Allt Robuic

START & FINISH: *Glenbranter Forestry car park*

DISTANCE: *4km; 2.5 miles*

TIME: *1hr 15mins*

MAP: *OS 56, 63; Harvey LLTOA*

TERRAIN: *Waymarked roads, tracks and paths*

GRADE: *Easy*

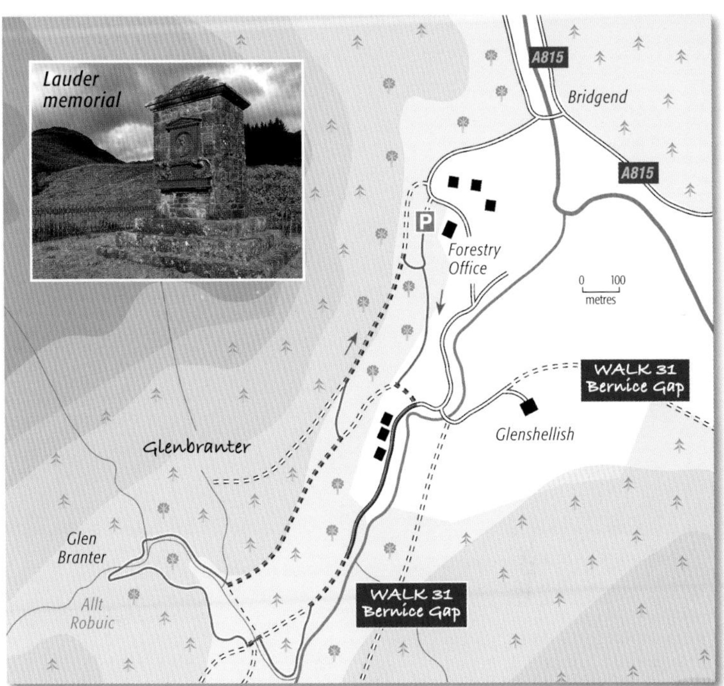

from the right, and traverse above forestry buildings into the glen. Follow a track left to the access road, then follow that up the glen, past a row of houses to where it becomes a track. Cross the bridge over the Allt Robuic, keeping right when the track forks and turn right almost immediately onto a yellow waymarked route up the concrete steps with a wooden balustrade. The path ascends via view-points and steps with glimpses through the trees to the waterfalls.

Cross a footbridge and follow the north bank of the burn to where it descends as an impressive waterfall before forcing its way between high cliffs of folded, contorted mica schist. Continue via steps and balustrades to gain the hillside and traverse above the main waterfall to a viewpoint.

At the waymarked junction follow the steps on the left to gain a forest track. Some distance down, leave the track for a path on the left which ascends steeply at first before levelling out to traverse the hillside. At the track junction turn right and descend to a waymarked path heading off right into the woodland above the forestry offices. Descend steeply then turn left back to the car park.

31 Bernice Gap

An ancient pass through the mountains

Bernice farmhouse and the Bernice Gap

By far the longest walk in this chapter, this outing follows an ancient route between the high peaks of Beinn Mhòr and Beinn Bheag. Almost all of the route is on good forest tracks, with only the short section through the pass itself on a mixture of open hillside and sheep paths.

From the Forestry Commission Scotland Glenbranter car park (NS 110 978). descend to the forestry offices and follow the access track south alongside the river to a junction. Turn left over the bridge to Glenshellish Farm and left again at the next junction to pass in front of and below the farmhouse.

Remain on this track above Loch Eck with fine views east to craggy Beinn Dubhain and later across the loch to the Whistlefield Inn at the Ardentinny road turning and **Sligrachan Hill** [33]. As Bernice farm is approached the view opens up directly south to the prominent small hill of Meall an t-Sìth, overlooking the open pasture surrounding the farm.

The track now descends towards Bernice farmhouse and a Y-junction with a white marker on the left. Turn right here – going left takes you straight down to the pasture below the house – and the track soon exits from the conifers with a view over the white farmhouse. Follow the forest track to its highest point, continuing straight ahead where the main track starts to bend left across a burn, to gain a short section of track which ends in bulldozed earth and stones.

Continue to the burn, cross over to gain its left back and follow a faint path up beside the forest edge. Go over the fence, follow it down right to regain the burn then follow that to the col at the

START & FINISH: *Glenbranter Forestry car park*

DISTANCE: *17.5km; 10.75 miles*

TIME: *5hrs 30mins*

MAP: *OS 56; Harvey LLTOA*

TERRAIN: *Tracks, paths and pathless hillside; rough and boggy in places*

GRADE: *Strenuous*

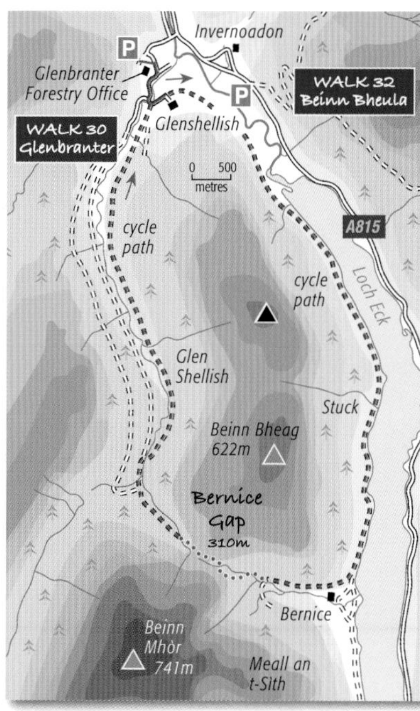

top of the pass.

The col is marshy, so cross over the fence on the right before you get there, to gain higher and drier ground between the two fence-lines. This leads to a gap in the fence from where a rough ATV track leads straight down and left to a burn and a firebreak in the conifers. Cross the burn to gain a firm forest track which re-crosses the burn then ascends to an area of felled woodland.

From here the forest track curves round and heads straight down to a track junction at the head of Glen Shellish. From here all tracks lead back to Glenbranter, but the best and most interesting is continuing straight ahead. At the next junction cross the burn on a small concrete bridge and follow the track above the east side of the river to a T-junction. A left turn leads down to the bridge below Glenshellish Farm and the track back to the start.

Loch Eck from the Bernice Gap

32 Beinn Bheula

Caisteal Dubh – the Black Castle of Cowal

Caisteal Dubh

Beinn Bheula dominates the high ground between Loch Eck and Loch Goil and is most frequently ascended from Lochgoilhead. An approach from Invernoaden, however, offers what is arguably a more interesting and unusual ascent, which can be linked with two smaller satellite hills to produce a satisfying round.

Park in the signposted layby on the west side of the A815 just beyond Invernoaden and the signposted Lauder memorial (NS 121 975). Walk south on the road for a short way to a track on the left signposted Forestry Commission Scotland Invernoaden.

Follow the track past a signpost indicating the 12km (7.5 mile) Right of Way to Lochgoilhead and a wooden post with a white waymark, the round Loch Eck cycle route. Ascend the gated track to a bend with views south over Loch Eck to **Sligrachan Hill** [33] and west over the River Cur to Glenbranter. The track now bends left then right – passing the return route coming in

Beinn Bheula from the bridge below Coire Ealt

START & FINISH: *Layby car park on A815 beyond Invernoaden*

DISTANCE: *13.5km; 8.25 miles*

TIME: *4hrs 30mins*

MAP: *OS 56; Harvey LLTOA*

TERRAIN: *Tracks and pathless hillside; boggy in places*

GRADE: *Strenuous*

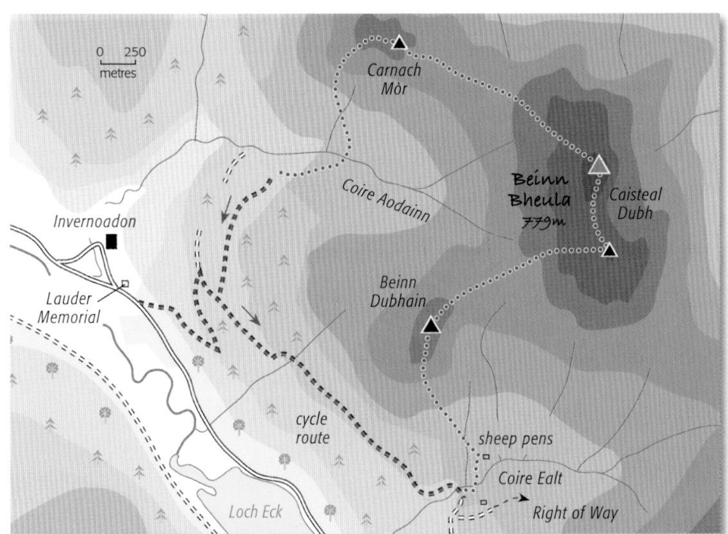

from the left – before leveling out and contouring south-east above Loch Eck, until it turns sharply east to cross the Coire Ealt burn at a bridge.

Straight after the bridge turn left and follow the right side of the fence – initially marshy – above the right bank of the burn. Go over a fence, drop down to the burn and cross it, then climb the hillside right of a secondary burn to old sheep pens marked on the Ordnance Survey 1:25,000 and Harvey maps. It is worth noting that the sign-posted Right of Way starts just beyond the bridge and appears a better approach to Beinn Bheula. But contrary to what is implied, it is only a route to Lochgoilhead. There is no path and the ground is very marshy. Ascend beside the burn, cross over and gain the top of Beinn Dubhain, which is significantly closer than it appears. Go over the craggy top of the hill, descend north-east to the col keeping left of the boggiest ground and continue to Beinn Bheula's southern top, or to the col separating it from the summit above Caisteal Dubh, the Black Castle. From the summit trig point, fine views can be had north-east to the Arrochar Alps and south to Beinn Mhòr and **Beinn Ruadh** [**39**], with the Isle of Arran beyond.

Follow the ridge north then west to Carnach Mòr which has a large area of collapsed cliffs and caves on its western flanks. From here descend south-west into Coire Aodainn – marshy in places – cross the burn and ascend to a forestry fence with a gate (NS 13157 98357). Go through and follow a clear path down beside the fence to a hidden track into the forest, which leads to the main track above the bends.

33 Sligrachan Hill

A small but commanding hill above Loch Eck

Sligrachan Hill from Loch Eck

Although really just the northern top of Beinn Ruadh, Sligrachan Hill is sufficiently characterful and far away from the main summit to be a distinct peak in its own right. It is easily climbed from the road over to Ardentinny, allowing the first 150m of the hill to be ascended in the car!

From Loch Eck follow the Ardentinny road to a point after a section of crash barrier on the left, where the cycle route crosses the road with gates on both sides, (NS 150 923). Park on the left by the large gate making sure you do not obstruct access. Parking is also possible lower down where the gated forest track followed by the cycle route continues above Loch Eck.

Cross the road and through a gate and follow the cycle route up to join the main track which comes up from the lower forest gate. Turn left and follow the track which descends slightly to where it forks. Turn right onto a grassier track and follow this as it ascends, with Sligrachan Hill starting to appear ahead.

The track ends at a turning spot and from its left end a grassy path leads off to the left. Cross a burn and keep ascending on a fairly clear path which leads up and round to gain a wide grassy firebreak beside the burn. Follow the firebreak for a short distance, then where another burn comes in from the left to join it, veer up and left. Ascend another firebreak to open hillside at the top, via a well-worn sheep path beside a burn. Continue beside the burn to pass easily over a fence and gain the first rocky knoll offering fine views north over Loch Eck to Loch Fyne.

START & FINISH: *Off-road parking on the Ardentinny road*

DISTANCE: *5.5km; 3.5 miles*

TIME: *2hrs 15mins*

MAP: *OS 56; Harvey LLTOA*

TERRAIN: *Tracks, paths and pathless hillside; boggy in places*

GRADE: *Easy / Moderate*

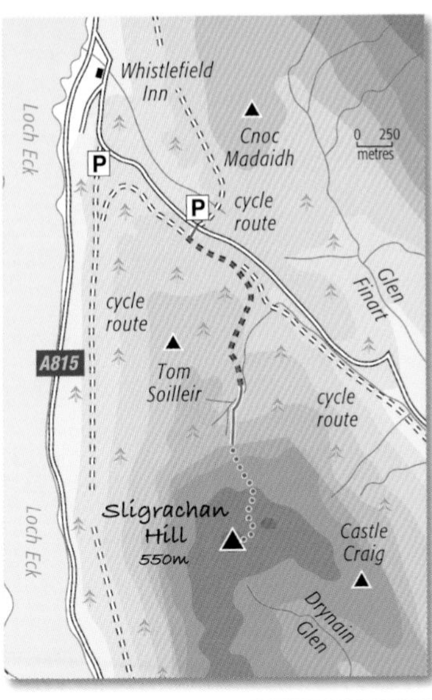

The prominent summit marker cairn

Sligrachan Hill lies straight ahead and is marked by a prominent old marker cairn on the summit. To the south, **Beinn Ruadh** [39] looks a long way off, but can be climbed in another 1hr 15mins there and back if further exercise is required. Return by the same route.

Sligrachan Hill, centre in sunlight, from Beinn Ruadh, with Beinn Bheula in the distance

34 Finart Bay

Sand, sea and salt air at Ardentinny

Finart Bay

Glen Finart is an unexpected delight for the first time visitor. Enclosed on three sides by forest and mountains, the glen ends with a sandy beach and sea views. It isn't a remote spot, but lying off the beaten track, accessed by single track road from Loch Eck to the north or Strone to the south, it is relatively quiet. This route links a number of short waymarked trails to create a delightful and varied walk combining beach, mature conifer and broadleaf woodland and the Glen Finart River, starting from the large car park at the north end of beach, (NS 191 885). The white corrugated iron buildings at the entrance to the car park are the remains of HMS Armadillo, a land base for Royal Navy Commandos who trained on the beaches during the war.

From the far end of the car park follow signs to the Birchwood Walk, but continue on the shore path past the steps to views of Shepherd's Point and rocky White Bay first, then return to the steps at the edge of the car park. Ascend the steps keeping straight ahead, go round a building and ascend through beech, birch and oak to a good viewpoint out over Finart Bay to Ardentinny. Continue steeply to denser and darker conifer forest where felling has taken place, and back into broadleaf. A steep path descends to a track which is followed left back towards the entrance to the car park.

Turn right onto the road past the golden eagle tree stump carving and the bowling green to just before the road bridge over the River Finart, where a waymarked path heads off onto the gravel of the Riverside Walk. Follow this to its end, cross over the old

START & FINISH: *Forestry car park at north end of Finart Bay*

DISTANCE: *5.5km; 3.5 miles*

TIME: *1hr 30mins*

MAP: *OS 56; Harvey LLTOA*

TERRAIN: *Waymarked paths and tracks with interpretation boards*

GRADE: *Easy*

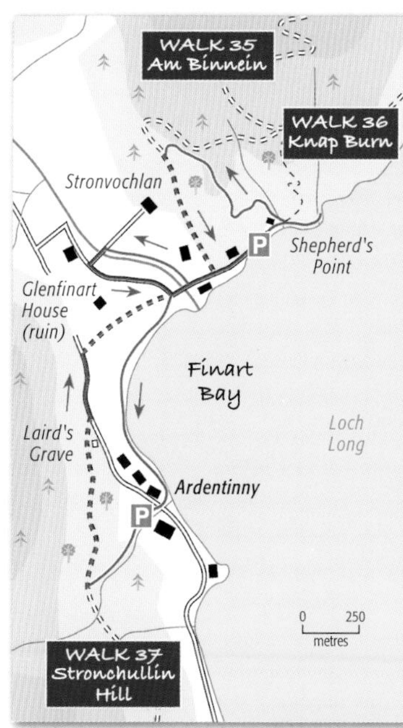

Arched Bridge, refurbished in 2005, and follow the quiet lane leftwards back to join the road just after the bridge.

Turn right then almost immediately left onto a waymarked path heading towards the shore which can be accessed at a picnic table on the left. The tower in the meadows on the right is the remains of Glenfinart House, which burned down in the late 1960s. Continue past all the houses to reach the main road and cross straight over and through the car park.

Ascend through conifer woodland at the back of Ardentinny Outdoor Centre to a forest track and follow it rightwards to a high point from where it descends to the 'Laird's Grave', commemorating Archibald Douglas Esquire, of Glenfinart who died in 1860. Continue down to the road and follow it left to a track on the right. Go round the gate and through the meadow with views up to the small hill of **Am Binnein** [35]. At its end, go round another gate to the road leading to the car park.

The old Arched Bridge over the River Finart

35 Am Binnein

A prominent hill and fine viewpoint

South down Loch Long to the Firth of Clyde

Am Binnein's prominent position above Finart Bay gives it spectacular sea views across Loch Long and the Clyde, which far outweigh any uphill effort required to reach its modest summit. Most of the route is on firm forest tracks and the open hillside is generally dry and grassy, but the section up the forest firebreak can be muddy in places.

From the car park at the north end of Finart Bay (NS 191 885), walk back to the road, turn right onto a track and ascend past the Discovery Trail car park and a gate to arrive at a track junction. Turn left and weave up the hillside, with increasingly good views. Go left at the next major track junction, the route from **Knap Burn** [36] comes in from the right, and continue ascending round the west side of Am Binnein to an obvious wide firebreak which appears barred by conifers at the top. Follow the firebreak to its top where a distinct animal track, hidden from below, leads right along the line of an old fence to gain the open hillside and fine views down to Glen Finart and Finart Bay.

START & FINISH: *Forestry car park at north end of Finart Bay*

DISTANCE: *9.5km; 6 miles*

TIME: *3hrs 15mins*

MAP: *OS 56; Harvey LLTOA*

TERRAIN: *Tracks, paths and pathless hillside; boggy in places*

GRADE: *Moderate*

Aim diagonally up and left to gain a broad shoulder and follow it to the summit, just south of an electricity pylon. Loch Long dominates the view, confined to the north by the Arrochar Alps and Luss Hills, but bursting out into the Firth of Clyde to the south. Westwards at the head of Glen Finart is **Beinn Ruadh** [39], with its southerly spurs descending to Loch Long to culminate in the rounded tops of **Stronchullin Hill** [37]and distant **Strone Hill** [45].

A return is easily made from here back to Glen Finart, but the cairned summit of Cruach a' Chaise beyond is also easily gained; (2km, 1.25 miles, 30mins return). Keen hillwalkers wanting a more strenuous day can continue across a short boggy area to the fine top of Creachan Mòr with its sheltered trig point, and superb views of Carrick Castle, Ardgoil and Loch Goil. From here it is possible to descend to Loch Goil with a return South from Carrick Castle [29], creating a long and

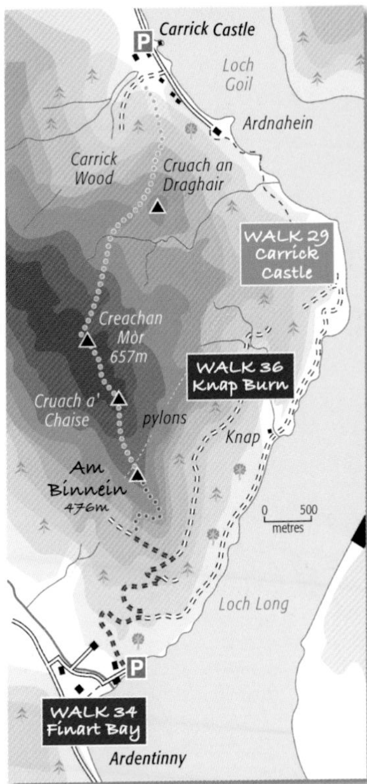

Am Binnein from Loch Long

satisfying circular route.

To continue to Carrick Castle, go north-west over Creachan Mòr's rocky top down to a small col, then descend the northern flanks of the mountain towards Carrick Castle and Cruach an Draghair. Skirt this top to its left, then descend northwards to gain the right edge of Carrick Wood and follow it down to a track leading right to the main road, south of the castle (approx 9km, 3hrs, Finart Bay to Carrick).

36 Knap Burn

RN commandos, submarines and seals

Coulport base from the Knap Burn

Loch Long's west shore provides the focus for this walk to the ruined farmstead below Knap Burn. With the Gare Loch further east, Loch Long is home to a large part of Britain's nuclear submarine fleet and the Navy base at Coulport features prominently on this walk. Not to be outdone by the human presence on the water, seals are also very common along this stretch of shoreline. From the car park at the north end of Finart Bay (NS 191 885), walk back towards the road. The white corrugated iron buildings at the entrance to the car park are the remains of HMS Armadillo, a land base for Royal Navy Commandos who trained on the beaches during the war. The foundations of other buildings can be traced in the undergrowth nearby.

Turn right onto a track and ascend past the Discovery Trail car park and a gate to arrive at a track junction, as for **Am Binnein** [35]. Continue right and follow the waymarked track which contours round the flanks of Am Binnein, descending towards the shore of Loch Long. Sections of the conifer forest hereabouts have been felled in recent years, but a ribbon of broadleaf

START & FINISH: *Forestry car park at north end of Finart Bay*

DISTANCE: *10.5km; 6.5 miles*

TIME: *3hrs*

MAP: *OS 56; Harvey LLTOA*

TERRAIN: *Waymarked tracks and paths*

GRADE: *Easy*

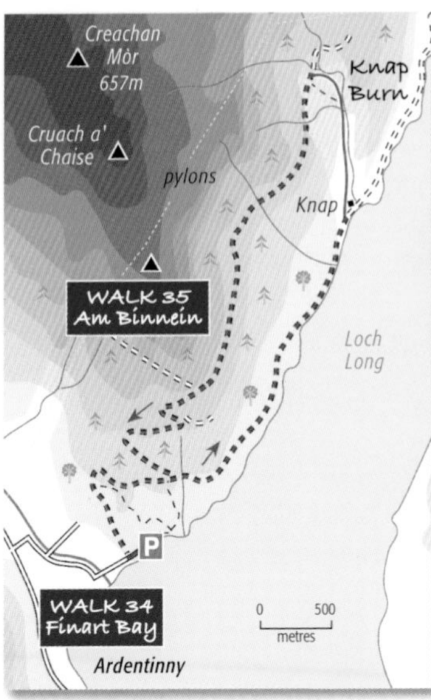

woodland lines the shore and fills the gaps between felling.

The Royal Naval installations north of Coulport on the opposite side of the loch soon make their presence known via the steady hum and rumble of machinery. Beyond the Naval base, and just before the ruined and overgrown building of Knap (NS 204 907) at the foot of the Knap Burn, leave the main track for a waymarked path on the left.

This path zigzags up the felled hillside to the left of the burn to reach a higher forestry track. Turn left onto this and follow it back south, contouring above the loch then gently ascending to round Am Binnein's south ridge, where the track divides. Turn left – the right turn is utilised on the ascent of Am Binnein – and follow the track as it zigzags down the hillside to the junction above the gate and the car park below.

Memorials at HMS Armadillo

37 Stronchullin Hill

Beinn Ruadh's southern satellite

Greenock and the Clyde from the flanks of Stronchullin Hill

Stronchullin Hill is the highest of the southern satellite peaks of Beinn Ruadh and is easily climbed from Ardentinny via forest tracks. It lacks a well-defined summit, but like **Am Binnein** [35] to the north and **Strone Hill** [45] to the south, the spectacular seascape of Loch Long and the Firth of Clyde far outweighs any aesthetic considerations over its shape.

Park at Ardentinny at the south end of Finart Bay, beside Ardentinny Outdoor Centre, (NS 187 875). From the back of the car park follow the path through conifer woodland to a junction, as for **Finart Bay** [34]. Turn left and keep left where the track divides. Continue up through forestry, passing an aerial and ignoring all turns, to emerge at a gate and stile with views south over Stronchullin Farm.

Continue for short distance and turn right onto the second grassy track (the first leads to a ruined building), just after a solitary silver birch and a rowan tree. Ascend the track following marker posts to gain a higher track at a gate. Cross over and the track divides. Turn left and follow the track uphill, heading for the glen south of Stronchullin Hill.

At a wide turning area, just before the track enters the forest, an obvious wide path ascends the hillside on the right. Follow this steeply up to a gate where the forest ends and exit onto the open hillside and excellent views. Remain on the track to where it fades and gain the broad grassy south-east ridge of Stronchullin Hill with fine views to Greenock and Glasgow, the Campsie Fells, Luss Hills and Arrochar Alps.

Continue to a fence and gate (NS 17765 85900) and then on up the broad ridge to the rounded summit and fine views south to Arran. The top is marked by little, save heavy rings which must have secured something like an aerial in the past. Not surprisingly, **Beinn Ruadh** [39] dominates the view to the north. Follow the broad north

START & FINISH: *Car park at Ardentinny*

DISTANCE: *13km; 8 miles*

TIME: *4hrs*

MAP: *OS 56; Harvey LLTOA*

TERRAIN: *Tracks, paths and pathless hillside; boggy in places*

GRADE: *Moderate / Strenuous*

ridge towards Beinn Ruadh, then swing round west and descend to the pylons and powerlines. A good track starts downhill from the pylons at NS 16502 86516 and leads down to fords and a junction with another track which comes in from the opposite side of the glen. Turn left and follow the track to a gate, beyond which it divides.

Turn left again and follow the track round the upper reaches of the glen with fine views out over the Clyde to arrive back at the wide turning area. Reverse the outward route back to Ardentinny.

North up Loch Long to the Arrochar Alps

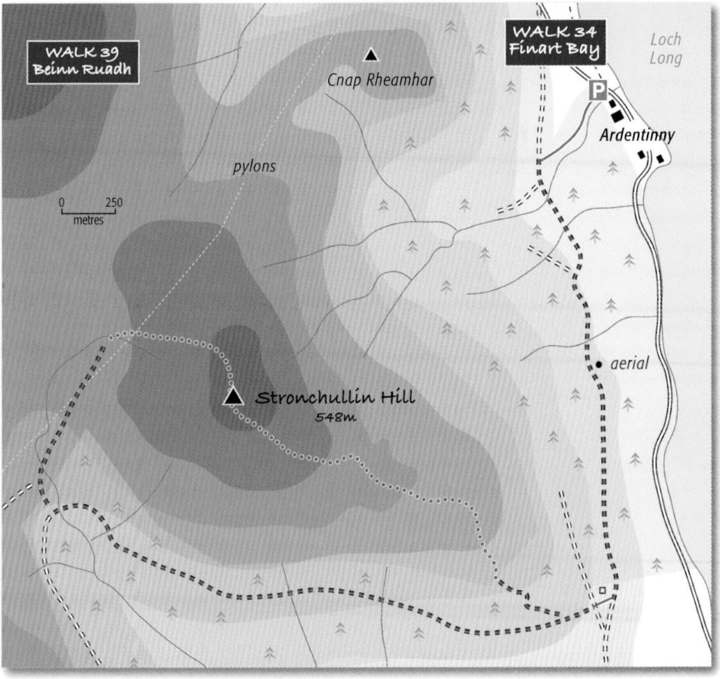

WALK 39 Beinn Ruadh

WALK 34 Finart Bay

Loch Long

Cnap Rheamhar

P

Ardentinny

pylons

0 250 metres

aerial

Stronchullin Hill 548m

Stronchullin Hill, left in shadow, from Strone Hill. Immediately to its left is Beinn Ruadh. To the right are Beinn Bheula and Am Binnein, with the Arrochar Alps in the distance

38 Inverchapel Birchwood

A short, steep ascent rewarded with fine views

Clach Bheinn from the upper path

In recent years a network of long distance cycle routes have been created in the vicinity of Loch Eck and Ardentinny, combining old forestry tracks and specially-laid cycle paths.

The routes have also significantly improved access for walkers, and this is the case at Inverchapel where a new footbridge over the Inverchapel Burn now links to a waymarked trail through the birch woodland on the south-west flanks of **Beinn Ruadh** [39].

This woodland offers a short, but steep ascent to a rocky knoll overlooking the south end of Loch Eck, with open views north to Beinn Mhòr and Glenbranter and south over Strath Eachaig and **Benmore Botanic Garden** [40]. The first section of the route is utilised in the ascent of Beinn Ruadh.

Looking across Strath Eachaig to A' Chruach

START & FINISH: *Inverchapel Forestry car park on A815*

DISTANCE: *2.5km; 1.5 miles*

TIME: *45mins*

MAP: *OS 56; Harvey LLTOA*

TERRAIN: *Waymarked tracks and paths*

GRADE: *Easy*

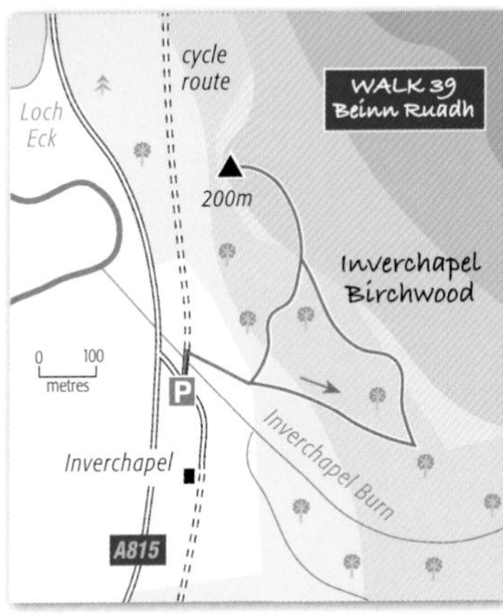

Start at the Forestry Commission Scotland Inverchapel car park on the east side of the A815, opposite Stratheck Caravan Park, (NS 145 864).

Cross the bridge over the Inverchapel Burn, turn right onto the waymarked circular path and ascend above the burn. Continue straight ahead where the path divides, the left-hand path is the return route, and climb steeply to a bench and viewpoint. From here the path traverses the hillside above the birch woodland with fine views across to rocky Clach Bheinn and Beinn Mhòr beyond.

Shortly after passing through a wooden kissing gate, the other path joins from below and a second kissing gate is reached. Go through this and on to where the path ends at the viewpoint over Loch Eck. The viewpoint is close to steep cliffs and care should be taken with young children.

Return to the path junction and zigzag down the right-hand path to complete the loop.

Clach Bheinn and Loch Eck from the viewpoint

39 Beinn Ruadh

An unfrequented hill with extensive views

Approaching the summit , Beinn Bheula in the distance

The highest point of a long upland area stretching from Sligrachan Hill in the north to Stronchullin Hill in the south, Beinn Ruadh holds a significant position at the southern end of Loch Eck, offering fine views the length of the loch and south over the Clyde from Glasgow to Arran. In the past, forest plantations have made access tricky, but the creation of waymarked walks at **Inverchapel** [38], have now alleviated this problem.

Start at the signposted Forestry Commission Scotland Inverchapel car park on the east side of the A815, (NS 145 864). Cross over the bridge, turn right onto a circular waymarked path and ascend alongside the Inverchapel Burn. Where the path divides, turn left and zigzag up to join an upper path.

Turn left and follow the path towards the viewpoint over Loch Eck. Just before a kissing gate and fence turn right to gain the open hillside – relatively bracken free in summer – ascending via assorted animal tracks to a fence. Cross

START & FINISH: *Inverchapel Forestry car park on A815*

DISTANCE: *6.5km; 4 miles*

TIME: *3hrs*

MAP: *OS 56; Harvey LLTOA*

TERRAIN: *Waymarked paths and pathless hillside*

GRADE: *Moderate / Strenuous*

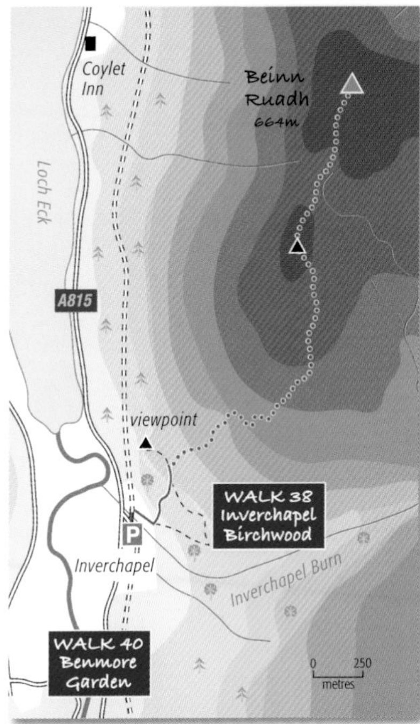

over this and traverse steeply up and right until clear of the craggier and steeper sections of Beinn Ruadh's south-east face.

Once clear of these, a leftward line gains Beinn Ruadh's south ridge with fine views west across **Benmore Garden** [40] to Loch Eck and Beinn Mhòr. To the south, rounded **Stronchullin Hill** [37] dominates the view, with **Strone Hill** [45] and the Clyde beyond.

A cairn marks Beinn Ruadh's south top, from where the summit trig point can be seen further to the north. An intermittent old fenceline can be followed along the knobbly ridge to the summit which offers fine views north to **Beinn Bheula** [32], distant Ben Cruachan, the Arrochar Alps and Ben Lomond.

It is worth continuing north a little from the summit for views across to the lochan below **Sligrachan Hill** [33], and east to **Finart Bay** [34] and Ardentinny. Return by the route of ascent.

Beinn Ruadh from Benmore Garden

40 Benmore Botanic Garden

Outstanding botanics in a mountain setting

A' Chruach from the upper track

This outstanding mountainside garden is one of Scotland's four National Botanic Gardens and the result of more than a century of scientific cultivation. Until recently known as the Younger Botanic Garden, the Benmore estate was given to the nation by HG Younger in 1928 and the 120 acre garden subsequently became an outstation of the Royal Botanic Garden Edinburgh (RBGE).

To describe a walk around Benmore Garden in detail would be restrictive and visitors should be free to explore at will. The following outlines a rough route which starts at the redwood avenue beyond the entrance. These giant sequoia were planted in 1863 by the then owner, American Piers Patrick. With an estimated lifespan of 3,500 years and maximum height of 91m (300ft), Benmore's redwoods still have a few years of life left in them!

Following the main track round to the left leads past Benmore House, now an outdoor centre, to the Glen Masson road. Continuing west leads round to the ruined Fernery on the right. This was part of the extensive garden devel-

The Formal Garden and Courtyard

START & FINISH: *Benmore Botanic Garden car park on A815*

DISTANCE: *Wander at will*

TIME: *All day*

MAP: *OS 56; Harvey LLTOA*

TERRAIN: *Tracks and paths with maps and interpretation boards*

GRADE: *Easy*

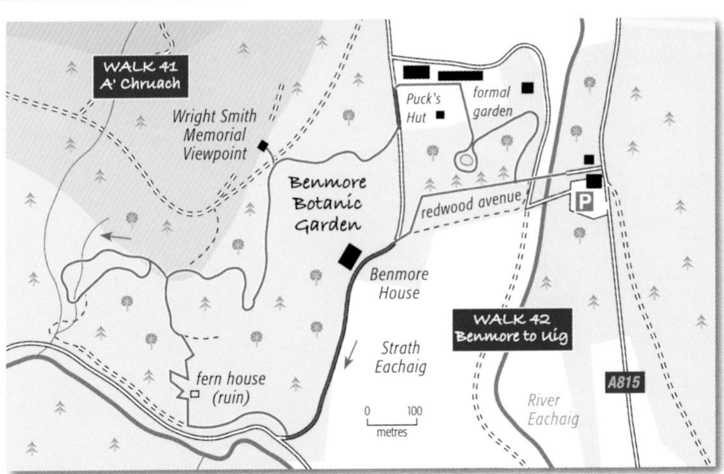

opment and tree planting instigated by wealthy Greenock sugar refiner James Duncan from 1870. Many of the trees outwith the immediate surroundings of Benmore House were planted for timber. Those within it, mixed with exotic shrubs, ferns and mosses, were planted for decoration. The garden sports more than 300 species of rhododendron. Climb up to the Fernery and continue through new planting to gain an upper track. Left from here offers good views up to **A' Chruach** [41] and the opportunity to explore the upper sections of the recently planted Chilean Rainforest Glade, and the Bhutanese Glade on the slopes below.

Returning to the upper path work your way east to the second northerly path, which leads to a gate in the boundary fence. The viewpoint on the other side of the track was built in 1990 to commemorate the life of Sir William Wright Smith, regius keeper at RBGE when Benmore became the western outstation and designed by Robin Lorimer. His grandfather Sir Robert Lorimer designed Puck's Hut in the Formal Garden, which was commissioned by HG Younger in the 1920s as a memorial to the previous RBGE regius keeper Issac Bayley Balfour and used to be sited in **Puck's Glen** [43].

From there head back into the garden and follow paths leftwards and down to a main path leading left to Benmore Courtyard, the main gatehouse and toilets. The Courtyard was purpose built as an art gallery in 1879 and continues to host exhibitions. Continue down into the Formal Gardens to explore Puck's Hut on the west side. Return to the centre of the garden and head towards the pond and the redwood avenue beyond. The main focus of attention here is the 1875 sculpture fountain 'Boy With Two Dolphins' in the centre of the pond. Continue on through trees and the redwood avenue to the bridge and back to the visitor centre and cafe.

Beinn Ruadh, left, from the Wright Smith Memorial above Benmore Garden

41 A' Chruach

An easily accessed small hill with a fine view

A' Chruach and Benmore House

A' Chruach overlooks the south end of Loch Eck and is easily accessed from Benmore via forest tracks. At about 480m it isn't a paticularly high hill, but its prominent position gives it an excellent view over Strath Eachaig and Holy Loch.

From the Benmore Botanic Garden car park cross the bridge over the River Eachaig and turn right to pass below the footbridge giving pedestrian access to Benmore Garden. Follow the road round the back of the stable block to the main gates, then round to the right.

Just short of Benmore Home Farm turn sharp left onto another track and ascend the hillside following the upper boundary fence of Benmore Garden, passing the gazebo style Wright Smith Memorial. The track then swings away from the boundary, heading round into Glen Massan.

Leave this track at the first turning on the right to ascend a steeper grassy track climbing the southern flanks of A' Chruach to a gate and stile on the right, marking the upper boundary of the forest plantations. Cross over to open hillside and follow a series of old fence posts directly to the summit.

To the south the view extends over Sandbank at the head of Holy Loch to Greenock and the prominent chimney at Inverkip on the north shore of the Firth of Clyde. Directly north from A' Cruach lies the impressive rocky top of Clach Bheinn, while to the north-west, a broad grassy ridge rises in a series of knolls over Creachan Beag to the distant summit of Beinn Mhòr. This 'Big Mountain' is the bulkiest and highest hill west of Loch Eck, but the summit is just a high point in a large expanse of rough moorland and it lacks the character and views of some of the

START & FINISH: *Benmore Botanic Garden car park on A815*

DISTANCE: *6.5km; 4 miles*

TIME: *2hrs 30mins*

MAP: *OS 56; Harvey LLTOA*

TERRAIN: *Tracks and pathless hillside; boggy in places*

GRADE: *Easy / moderate*

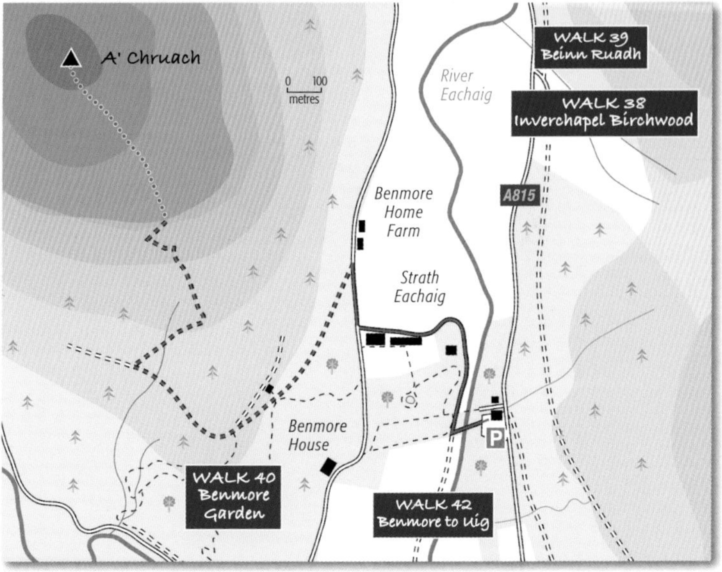

A' Chruach
0 100 metres
River Eachaig
WALK 39 Beinn Ruadh
WALK 38 Inverchapel Birchwood
A815
Benmore Home Farm
Strath Eachaig
Benmore House
WALK 40 Benmore Garden
WALK 42 Benmore to Uig
P

surrounding, lesser peaks.

Walkers wanting a little more exercise can continue north-west on the broad grassy ridge to the first craggy knoll south of Creachan Beag. This knoll is marked with a distinctive cairn and offers similar views to A' Chruach, from a slightly more elevated perspective.

A' Chruach and Benmore Home Farm from the east

42 Benmore to Uig

Strath Eachaig's big trees

River Eachaig and Strath Eachaig

Along with his plantings at Benmore, landowner James Duncan was responsible for most of the redwood planting along Strath Eachaig in the late 19th century. In a concentrated programme more than 6.5 million native and foreign conifers and broadleaves were planted on the Benmore and Kilmun estates and more than 130 years later, many of these Douglas and silver firs and giant sequoia have become an integral part of the landscape.

This walk starts along the River Eachaig before ascending the east side of Strath Eachaig through more recent conifer planting. The route back to Benmore then descends through the old plantings with ample opportunity to admire the giant redwoods.

From the Benmore Botanic Garden car park cross the bridge over the River Eachaig, turn left onto a track and follow it south beside the river with views north across Strath Eachaig to Benmore House. At a sharp bend in the track leave it on the left for a metal footbridge over the river. The track continues to meet the Glen Massan road at the Deer Park Cottages.

Pass the wooden Uig Hall to the access road and main road beyond. Cross straight over to another access road, which leads to the old road between Puck's Glen and Benmore Garden, now bypassed by the A815. Turn right and almost immediately left onto a waymarked path into the forest. Climb steeply through the forest taking advantage of various benches en route to admire the foxgloves and rhododendrons to arrive at a modern forestry

START & FINISH: *Benmore Botanic Garden car park on A815*

DISTANCE: *4km; 2.5 miles*

TIME: *1hr 30mins*

MAP: *OS 56; Harvey LLTOA*

TERRAIN: *Tracks and waymarked paths; steep and muddy in places*

GRADE: *Easy*

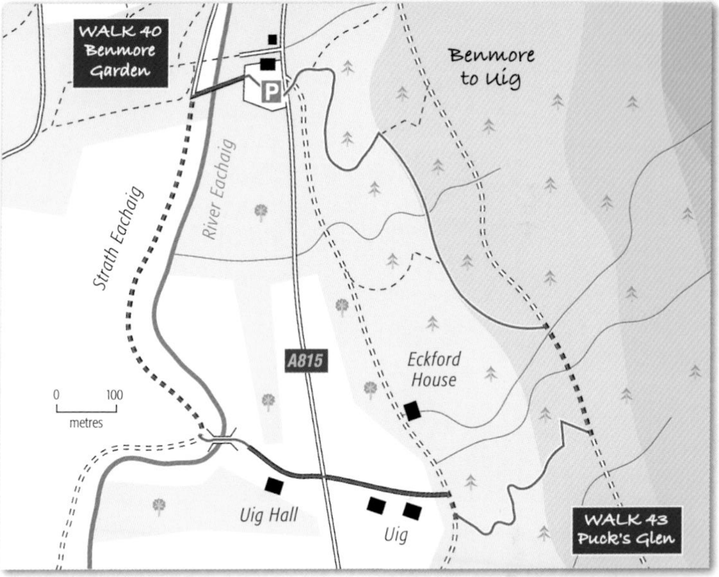

WALK 40 Benmore Garden

Benmore to Uig

River Eachaig

Strath Eachaig

A815

Eckford House

0 100 metres

Uig Hall

Uig

WALK 43 Puck's Glen

track, a continuation of the one utilised at **Puck's Glen** [43].

Go left onto the track which offers views to the mountains through the trees and continue to a waymarked path on the left signposted to the Black Gates. Descend then contour through the forest, continuing straight on where the waymarked path starts a steep descent to the left. This high path joins a second path descending from the track above and follows it down.

Cross a large fallen silver fir via an ingenious stile and continue down through Douglas fir and western hemlock to giant sequoia and coastal redwoods to the Benmore car park. The success of many of these trees shows how well suited they are to the climate and soils of Strath Eachaig.

Wind-blown silver fir and stile

43 Puck's Glen

Magical landscape of moss, ferns and water

The tropical landscape of Puck's Glen

Narrow rocky gorges always make for spectacular walking and Puck's Glen is no exception. If you can pick a sunny day after rain when the paths are relatively dry, the volume in the burn is dramatically high and the abundant rainforest vegetation lusciously green, then you'll be getting the best of everything.

It's an exciting expedition regardless of the weather. Some paths have drops at their edge and need a little care, especially with youngsters in the wet, but steps have been cut into the rock in places and wooden footbridges keep you on the best and widest paths.

The walk starts from the Puck's Glen car park on the A815 south of Benmore, (NS 146 839). From the car park follow the tarmac road north past chalets on the left, to the entrance to Puck's Glen at a stone bridge and mile post. Descend the steps and follow the Lower Glen through a tropical landscape of ferns, moss-draped cliffs and waterfalls, on a path which crisscrosses over the burn.

Ascend the stone steps to a path junction. Turn left and descend back into the gorge – the ascending path continues to join the upper path (the return route). Continue the tour through the spectacular landscape of the Upper Glen, again crisscrossing the burn on footbridges, to reach steps leading out of the glen to a forest track.

Cross straight over to steps leading into the Top Glen and a slightly wilder landscape and less frequented path. At the top of the glen go left to a path signposted Black Gates (the gates and car park at Benmore Garden) and follow this down through conifer forest and felled areas to arrive at the forest track, signposted left to Puck's Glen and right to Black Gates.

Turn left and follow the track past a

START & FINISH: *Puck's Glen Forestry car park on A815*

DISTANCE: *5.5km; 3.5 miles*

TIME: *1hr 45mins*

MAP: *OS 63; Harvey LLTOA*

TERRAIN: *Tracks and paths; mostly waymarked*

GRADE: *Easy*

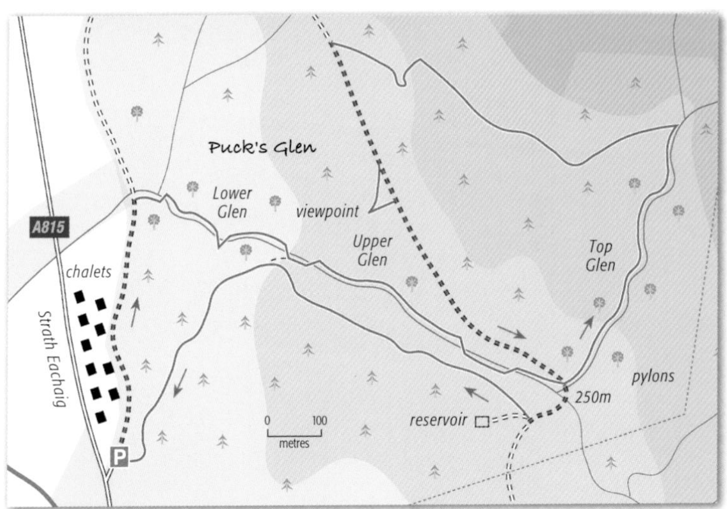

viewpoint with a lone pine tree, back to the top of the Upper Glen and on over a bridge (signposted Viewpoint) to a track on the right leading to an underground reservoir. Turn immediately right onto a path and descend above the glen – the waterfalls can be heard below – to meet the ascending path between Lower and Upper Glens. Continue the descent through woodland to the car park.

Decsending the Lower Gorge

44 Kilmun Arboretum

Exotic tree experiments on the Holy Loch

Sandbank from Kilmun

Although significant areas of forestry were planted in the 18th and 19th centuries on the Benmore and Kilmun estates, Kilmun Arboretum was established in the 1930s as an outdoor research experiment. With commercial forest planting gathering pace, foresters were anxious to know how well some tree species flourished on Scotland's west coast. What makes Kilmun unique, is that unlike other arboreta up and down the country, the 162 species of foreign and native trees were planted in separate groups across the 180 acre site. Twelve of these conifer species are now on the endangered species list and, in general, the conifers planted at Kilmun appear to have fared better than the broadleafs.

A walk round Kilmun transports the

Tasmanian eucalyptus

START & FINISH: *Kilmun Arboretum Forestry car park on A880*

DISTANCE: *3km; 1.75 miles*

TIME: *1hr*

MAP: *OS 56; Harvey LLTOA*

TERRAIN: *Waymarked paths with interpretation boards*

GRADE: *Easy*

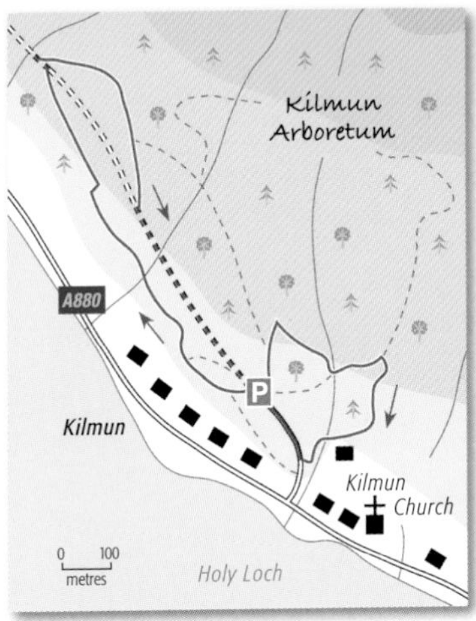

visitor through the forests of the world. Turn a corner and Himalayan spruce become Australian eucalyptus; turn another and you are surrounded by European oak and beech or North American Douglas firs or Wellingtonia.

Lack of funding in recent years resulted in a deterioration in the arboretum's paths, but this has been rectified, with new paths created and damaged areas repaired. The result is a slightly shorter walking route, but firmer and more durable paths.

From the main road in Kilmun follow the signs to the Forestry Commission Scotland car park, (NS 163 822). A red waymarked path descends from the bottom south-west corner of the car park and runs north-west above Kilmun. Houses and the views across the head of the Holy Loch to Sandbank are soon lost as the path weaves its way up through the airy woodland to arrive at a more open area of silver-barked Tasmanian eucalyptus.

A short distance further on the main track leading from the car park is reached. Turn left, then immediately right into a much more European habitat of dense oak and beech. Descend back to the track and follow it to the top of the car park. Turn left onto the blue waymarked path and ascend through massive Wellingtonia and redwoods, before descending to a burn and a path junction.

Turn left following the green waymark, cross the footbridge over the burn and ascend steps to a high point among swamp and bald Cyprus trees. From here the path descends through European birch, beech, ash and alder to emerge on the access road. Follow the access road back right to the car park.

Assorted other paths can be explored throughout the arboretum, however, many are boggy or blocked by fallen trees, so anyone steeping off the beaten track should go prepared for an adventurous bushwhack. In the future, some of these paths may be reinstated.

In the heart of the arboretum

45 Strone Hill

Hidden gem of the Cowal peninsula

Looking up the Clyde over Loch Long and Gare Loch to Glasgow beyond

This fine little hill faces Gourock and enjoys commanding views up Loch Long to **The Cobbler** [18] and the Arrochar Alps, as well as the length of the Clyde from Dumbarton Rock to Ailsa Craig. Despite the trig point on its lowly 385m summit, it isn't actually named on Ordnance Survey maps, but is known as Strone Hill after Strone village and Strone Point to its immediate south. It's a hidden gem of Dunoon and the Cowal peninsula.

The hill is easily accessed from parking on the A880 coastal road at the foot of High Road, which leads to the golf course behind Strone village, (NS 186 807). Ascend High Road for a short distance then turn left into Westfield road and follow this to where it ends at a forest track.

Follow the track to a junction and turn sharp right onto another track which ascends above the village and golf course. At a four-way junction turn left onto a path with a marker post and ascend through new plantations with fine views over the Clyde seascape.

The path then swings round passing various marker posts to meet a boundary wall beside older conifer forest. Ascend steeply beside the wall, then continue zigzagging up the hill-side, still on a well-marked wide path.

When the path appears to end, continue to the wall to gain a hidden path which follows the wall and then ascends the hillside. This is fairly wet and muddy to start, but soon leads to drier ground. Pass through a break in the wall and follow a firebreak to more open hillside. The old wall leads directly to the summit and spectacular views.

START & FINISH: *Car park on A880 at west end of Strone village*

DISTANCE: *8km; 5 miles*

TIME: *3hrs*

MAP: *OS 63; Harvey LLTOA*

TERRAIN: *Tracks, paths and pathless hillside; boggy in places*

GRADE: *Moderate*

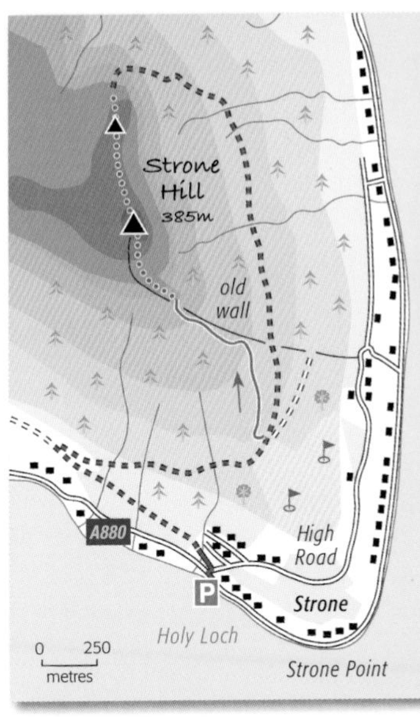

South to Great Cumbrae

Cross the moorland due north to the top of the next hill – named Blairbeg Hill on the OS 1:25,000 map – watching your step as the going is boggy in places, and descend the left side of the hill to a rough access track leading steeply down through the forest.

This track joins a more horizontal access track which is followed south back to the four way junction, from where you retrace your outward route back to the start.

Approaching the summit

Inveruglas & Inverarnan

Ben Lomond and cruise boats anchored at Inveruglas

North of Tarbet the winding A82 hugs the western shore of Loch Lomond, sharing a narrow strip between the mountains and the loch with the Oban and Fort William railway. As a consequence, general access from the road to these western hills can be awkward away from the small settlements along the route, where cars can be parked, and tracks give access to the hillsides and the glens leading west.

The first good access point beyond Tarbet is the lochside car park by the Sloy Power Station at Inveruglas. This has a cafe, public toilets and a pier and is a popular starting point for cruises on the loch. The car park also allows easy access to the locked road leading to the switching plant below Coire-grogain farm, the Loch Sloy dam and the steep south ridges of **Ben Vorlich** [46] and **Ben Vane** [48]. Part of this road also features in the round route through **Glen Loin** [16], described in the Tarbet & Arrochar chapter.

Ben Vorlich is often climbed from Ardlui, which is also accessible by train, unlike Inveruglas. However, the south ridge from Inveruglas allows the walker to explore a less-frequented aspect of this fine mountain. Ben Vane's south ridge is by far the most interesting route on the mountain and the most popular as a consequence.

Sloy was Scotland's first major hydro project and was swiftly followed by others throughout the Highlands as the

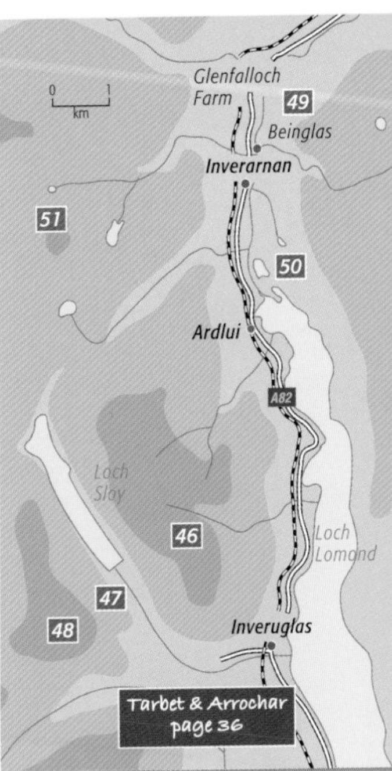

steady electrification of rural communities progressed throughout the 1950s. This massive engineering project involved transporting hundreds of thousands of tons of quarried aggregate, for use in the concrete for the dam wall, round the eastern flanks of Ben Vane. The route of the **Loch Sloy Conveyor** [47] can still be traced and offers an interesting high level walk.

Loch Lomond ends just beyond Ardlui where the land rises to meet Glen Falloch. Inverarnan grew up as a staging post on the cattle droving routes from Kintyre and the islands east to Loch Katrine and market at Falkirk and Crieff. Here the West Highland Way (WHW) emerges from the east side of Loch Lomond and is utilised by two walks. The first follows the WHW north into Glen Falloch before doubling back and ascending to a steep descent beside the fine **Eagle Falls** [49]. The second follows the WHW south to **Cnap Mòr** [50], a tiny isolated hill at the very head of Loch Lomond, with spectacular views south to Ben Lomond.

The final walk in this chapter returns to the hills for an ascent of secretive **Beinn Damhain** [51] on the park boundary. Although smaller than the peaks that surround it, Beinn Damhain far outstrips them in character and solitude, while offering good views south to Ben Vorlich and north to magnificent Ben Lui. The hill is easily accessed by tracks from Glenfalloch Farm.

GETTING THERE

Road: *From Glasgow & Edinburgh – M8, A82. From Stirling – A811, A82*

Train: *Scotrail from Glasgow Central (08457 484950), <www.firstgroup.com>*

Bus: *See pages 10 & 11*

TOWNS & VILLAGES

Inveruglas: *Shop, cafe, public toilets (01301 704392)*

Ardlui: *Shop, hotels, restaurants*

Inverarnan: *Hotels, cafe*

ACCOMMODATION

Centred on Ardlui, but scattered hotel and bed and breakfast available up the west shore of Loch Lomond. Campsites at Beinglas and Ardlui. See also pages 10 & 11

46 Ben Vorlich

A less frequented route up a popular mountain

Looking down the south ridge to Ben Lomond

Ben Vorlich is an extensive mountain, which can be climbed from a number of directions. Ardlui to the east is one of the most popular starting points, but Inveruglas to the south offers quicker and easier access, as well as an opportunity to ascend the long and less-frequented south ridge.

From the large Inveruglas car park just north of Sloy Power Station, follow the signposted path past the power station back to the padlocked access road to Coiregrogain farm and Loch Sloy dam. Go through the kissing gate and follow the road under the railway bridge. It is possible to take a short cut on the left almost immediately after the bridge, onto a path which ascends beside the Inveruglas Water to meet the access road after the big bend. This passes through pleasant woodland, but can be very boggy in places.

After the initial ascent from Loch Lomond, the access road levels out below the broad frontal face of Ben Vorlich's south ridge. A burn with scattered trees in its lower reaches lies in the centre of the face and the route ascends to the right of this burn. There are scattered animal paths, but no established path and it is not as steep as it looks from below.

At the electricity substation, turn right onto a subsidiary access road which traverses eastwards across the hillside below the face. Gain the hillside as soon as possible beyond the burn and ascend steadily up grassy and heathery slopes with some bracken and animal tracks to gain the broad upper ridge where the ground levels out. The ascent gives fine views east to Loch Lomond, Inversnaid and Ben Ledi beyond, west to **Ben Vane** [48], **Beinn Chorranach** [23] and Beinn Ìme and

START & FINISH: *Inveruglas car park on the A82*

DISTANCE: *13km; 8 miles*

TIME: *4hrs 30mins*

MAP: *OS 56; Harvey LLTOA*

TERRAIN: *Tracks, paths and pathless hillside; rocky in places*

GRADE: *Strenuous*

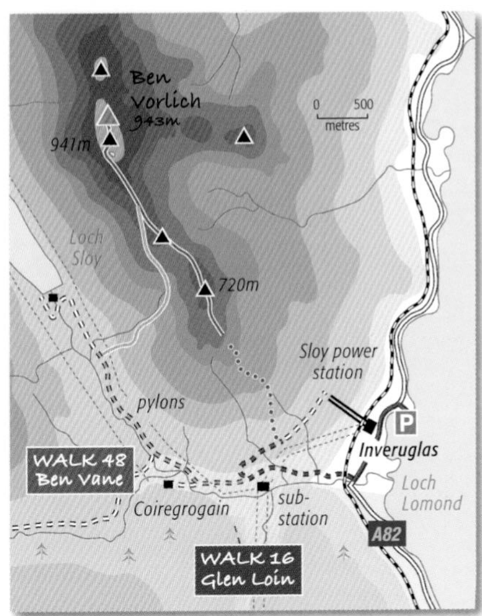

south to **Cruach Tairbeirt** [13].

Once the ridge is gained a path leads north over a series of knobbly tops towards the summit. The most enjoyable route takes the ridge direct, although the rockier sections can be bypassed by a path on the right.

Beyond the second top, the route joins the well-worn path ascending from Loch Sloy, and becomes much wider, continuing through a wide trough created by a massive landslip on the west face, to arrive at a tiny lochan below the craggy summit.

The main path continues to the left, but the most direct and straightforward route is by sticking to the high ground further right. Here a lesser path skirts to the right of the small crag, gains the ridge and leads directly to the trig point on the south top. From here, continue along the ridge to ascend to the summit (2 m higher), which is marked by a cairn on a small crag.

A return may be made by reversing the line of ascent, or (longer) descending via the Loch Sloy path to the access road. The top of this path is steep and eroded with some scrambly sections, while the bottom is quite boggy. The access road leads back to the electricity substation.

The south top, from the tiny lochan

47 Loch Sloy Conveyor

The birth of Scottish hydro power

Cutting for the Loch Sloy Conveyor, from the Ben Vane path

Opened on October 18th 1950, Sloy Power Station was the first major hydro plant in the Highlands and can rightly be called the birth place of hydroelectric power in Scotland. Heralded as the end to post war blackouts, the saviour of heavy industry on the Clyde and the electrifier of the Highlands, hydro fever was soon rippling through the upland glens. The losers at Sloy were Clan MacFarlane whose homeland round the loch was covered with concrete, gallons of water and electricity pylons, despite the clan's motto; 'Loch Sloy, This I'll Defend'.

During the building a conveyor transported the 300,000 tons of aggregate required for the dam concrete from the quarry in Coiregrogain on the south side of Ben Vane, round the mountain to the dam site on the east side. Shown as a footpath on the Ordnance Survey 1:25,000 map, the route is marked in places by wooden poles, supporting buttress walls, old wooden sleepers and metal work and cuttings blasted through the rocky hillside. It is indistinct and boggy in places, but has an exploratory feel which anyone interested in the archaeological history of Scotland's mountains will appreciate.

From Inveruglas car park just north of Sloy Power Station, follow the previous route to the electricity substation and continue on the road to the foot of the dam, passing a waymarked left turning to Coiregrogain farm and **Glen Loin** [**15**] and a track junction with a bridge, at the foot of **Ben Vane** [48]. Pass below the dam and ascend to where it bends sharply right towards a tunnel.

Climb over the crash barrier on the left and head diagonally down aiming for a point just below an old telegraph pole, to pick up a faint grassy track leading to a burn and a small sleeper footbridge marked on the OS map.

Beyond this a more obvious section

START & FINISH: *Inveruglas car park on the A82*

DISTANCE: *13.5km; 8.25 miles*

TIME: *3hrs 45mins*

MAP: *OS 56; Harvey LLTOA*

TERRAIN: *Roads, tracks and paths; boggy in places*

GRADE: *Moderate*

on a raised embankment is gained. Ascend along various sections of raised wall and bank to cross a burn into a marshy area (marked ford on the map), where the route becomes fainter. Remain on the same gently ascending line aiming for a large round rock on the skyline to pass through a small walled cutting marked by iron stakes and a solitary silver birch. After this the route is more entrenched with a few old sleepers here and there in the grass.

Pass below a prominent cliff and on to beyond the end of the crags. The route now turns sharply right to pass between two obvious boulders, heading for a notch left of the crags. At this point the track lies on an embankment, marked by scree debris below. If this sharp right is missed just continue traversing the hillside past a section of tussocky grass to a levelled area leading to a small dam and sluice on a burn.

The line of the conveyor is clear on the hillside just above. Cross the dry bed of the burn below the sluice and ascend to the conveyor track. The sharp right turn leads naturally to a level area, which leads round to the burn.

Loch Sloy Conveyor path and the hydro dam

Continue on the obvious track traversing the hillside, marked by wooden sleepers, cuttings, old walls and metal stakes to arrive at the Ben Vane path at an old iron stake, resembling a ram's horns. Follow the path downhill to a boggy level area at the col on the ridge then left more steeply down the side of the ridge to the burn. Cross over the burn to gain the track leading back to the road.

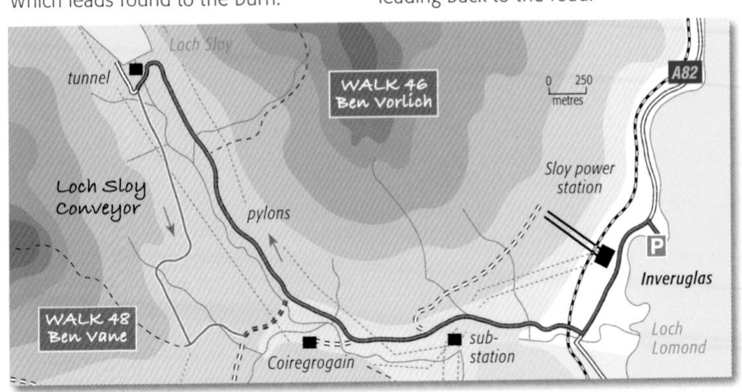

48 Ben Vane

Steep climbing, but well worth the effort

Ben Vane and the Inveruglas Water

Situated at the north end of the peaks known as the Arrochar Alps, Ben Vane offers a continually interesting and continuously steep ascent to a lofty summit with extensive views to the surrounding high mountains. It may be the steepest of the '3,000 foot' peaks in the area, but it is also the lowest and this combined with the comparatively gentle road approach from Inveruglas, makes Ben Vane an ascent worth persevering with.

From the large Inveruglas car park just north of Sloy Power Station, follow the signposted path past the power station back to the padlocked access road to Coiregrogain farm and Loch Sloy dam. Go through the kissing gate and follow the road under the railway bridge. It is possible to take a short cut on the left almost immediately after the bridge onto a path which ascends beside the Inveruglas Water to meet the access road after the big bend. This passes through pleasant woodland but can be very boggy in places.

After the initial ascent from Loch Lomond the road levels out below the south ridge of **Ben Vorlich [46]** and continues past an electricity substation linked to the Sloy hydro scheme and a waymarked turning down to Coiregrogain farm and **Glen Loin [15]**, to arrive at a track junction below Ben Vane's south-west ridge. Follow the track left over the bridge and ascend to a small bridge over a burn, just past a small disused quarry.

START & FINISH: *Inveruglas car park on the A82*

DISTANCE: *12km; 7.5 miles;*

TIME: *4hrs 30mins*

MAP: *OS 56; Harvey LLTOA*

TERRAIN: *Tracks and paths; boggy and rocky in places*

GRADE: *Strenuous*

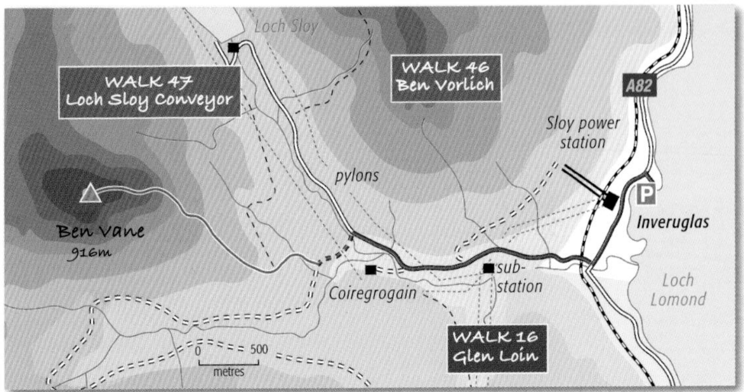

An obvious path leaves the track along the right side of the burn. Cross the burn and marshy ground left of the fenced enclosure marked on the Ordnance Survey 1:25,000 and Harvey maps, to gain and climb the ridge to its broad crest. From here the path continues at a gentle angle then steadily steepens, passing a prominent metal stake shaped like ram's horns, the line of the **Loch Sloy Conveyor** [47].

As height is gained progress ahead appears increasingly barred by steep cliffs of mica schist, but the path dramatically weaves between them avoiding any impasse. For the whole ascent Ben Lomond and Loch Lomond dominate the view to the east, while Ben Vorlich to the north grows in size as height is gained.

A couple of false summits raise expectations only to dash them again and just when you anticipate yet another disappointment, the path suddenly deposits you onto a small plateau leading to the summit cairn. Immediately to the west lie **Beinn Chorranach** [23] and the craggy north-east face of Beinn Ime. To the south **Beinn Narnain & A' Chrois** [17] dominate the view. Return by the outward route.

South ridge of Ben Vorlich

Ben Vane from Coiregrogain

49 Eagle Falls

A steady ascent to a waterfall and high viewpoint

Eagle Falls from Inverarnan

During prolonged spells of sub-zero temperatures in the 1980s and early '90s, the waterfall above Beinglas Farm froze solid, offering ice climbers some entertaining sport. In the absence of a name on the Ordnance Survey map, the climbers named them Eagle Falls and have known them by this ever since.

Other visitors know them as plain Ben Glas Falls after the Ben Glas Burn, although the Harvey map also names them Grey Mare's Tail. Exactly what the name is who knows, but Eagle Falls seems suitably inspiring, despite the fact that the falls have not frozen in recent years and the climbers have moved on to pastures new.

Parking is possible at Inverarnan on the A82, in the car park beside the Drovers Lodge and opposite the Drovers Inn, (NN 317 184). Follow the path beside the road, north to the sign-posted access road to Beinglas Farm and campsite. Cross the bridge over the River Falloch and continue towards the farmhouse, signposted bar and restaurant, with a good view towards the Eagle Falls. The road leads round to the right in front of the restaurant to a track at the back of the farm, the route of the West Highland Way (WHW). Turn left onto this and follow the track north as it ascends Glen Falloch. At a point where the path starts to descend slightly, an obvious grassy track branches off to the right. A short distance on from this another track joins from the left, an indication that you have gone too far.

Follow the grassy track as it zigzags up the hillside, with fine views of Glen Falloch, to arrive at a gate. Go through

START & FINISH: *Car park by Drovers Lodge, Inverarnan on A82*

DISTANCE: *6.5km; 4 miles*

TIME: *2hrs 30mins*

MAP: *OS 56; Harvey LLTOA*

TERRAIN: *Tracks and paths; some waymarks, wet and rough in places*

GRADE: *Easy / Moderate*

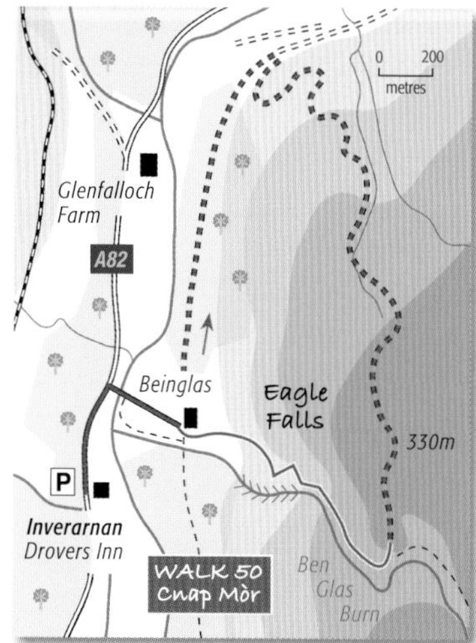

this, continuing to gain height, with views back north to **Ben Lui** [57] and Beinn Dubhchraig as they start to rise above Glen Falloch. Further north, **Ben Challum** [54] becomes visible above Strath Fillan.

Go over a ridge of high ground and descend to meet the old cattle drovers' route from Inverarnan to Loch Katrine in The Trossachs, and the path up to Beinn Chabhair to the east. The Ben Glas burn is very beautiful in its upper reaches with stretches of open water and many small waterfalls.

Turn right and follow the path steeply down into Glen Falloch. The path is continuously steep and eroded in places, with some rocky sections, which can be slippery in the wet. While the noise from the waterfall can be clearly heard, the waterfall itself is less easily seen and the upper section is fenced off to protect visitors and sheep from getting too close.

Cross the ladder stile at the bottom and go left round the chalets to pass through the camping ground to a stile. Cross over and skirt rightwards round the field to gain the access road before the bridge. Turn left and follow the road back to Inverarnan.

Ben Glas Burn

50 Cnap Mòr

A little big hill with an even bigger view

Looking north to Ben Lui, left, from the West Highland Way below Cnap Mòr

This craggy little hill combines an enjoyable section of the West Highland Way with a spectacular view down the narrow confines of Loch Lomond from Ardlui to Ben Lomond. The route is relatively straightforward and suitable for youngsters.

Parking is possible at Inverarnan on the A82, in the car park beside the Drovers Lodge and opposite the Drovers Inn, (NN 317 184). Follow the path beside the road, north to the signposted access road to Beinglas Farm and campsite. The road gives a good view to **Eagle Falls** [49], above the farm buildings. Cross the bridge over the River Falloch, immediately beyond which a signpost directs you right onto a link path to the West Highland Way (WHW).

Skirt the field, initially beside the river then alongside a burn, to a stile into the camping ground. Go through this onto a track and follow this rightwards to a footbridge over the Ben Glas Burn and the WHW. From here the path ascends steadily into broadleaf woodland of rowan, birch, hawthorn and oak.

Cross a stile and pass the old shielings and farm buildings at Blarstainge and continue south on the WHW with unfolding views to the small hill of Cnap Mòr, with the Dubh Lochan below. Arrive at a waymark on the WHW just as it meets a fence and starts

Cnap Mòr

START & FINISH: *Car park by Drovers Lodge, Inverarnan on A82*

DISTANCE: *6.5km; 4 miles*

TIME: *2hrs 30mins*

MAP: *OS 56; Harvey LLTOA*

TERRAIN: *Waymarked paths and pathless hillside*

GRADE: *Easy*

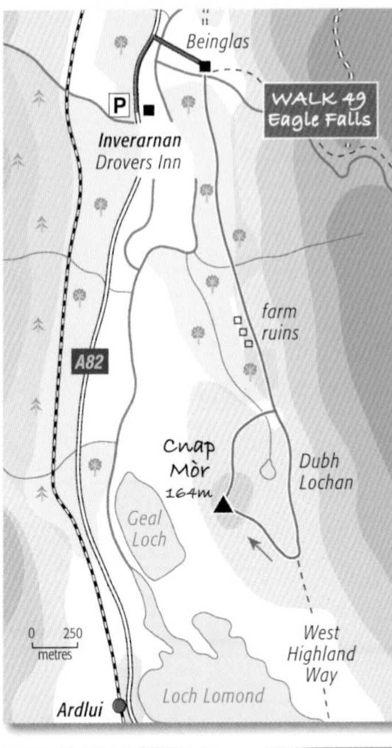

to descend to Ardleish and Loch Lomond.

Turn right here and follow a rough sheep path beside the old fence towards the summit of Cnap Mòr. This leads to a plateau area topped with a number of small hillocks, the highest lying to the north-west overlooking the Geall Loch and River Falloch and marked by a small cairn. This offers panoramic views west over Loch Lomond to Ardlui and **Ben Vorlich** [46] and south down the loch to Ben Lomond.

Continue round the summit plateau to descend the broad north ridge for a short way, then rightwards round the high ground enclosing the Dubh Lochan to its north, aiming for the pylons on the hillside above. Cross the small burn draining from the loch where it is closest to the WHW, gain the path and follow it back to Beinglas with fine views north to the shapely summit of **Ben Lui** [57], poking its head above the hills flanking Glen Falloch.

Dubh Lochan from the north ridge of Cnap Mòr

Looking down Loch Lomond to Ben Lomond from Cnap Mòr

51 Beinn Damhain

An isolated and unexpectedly rocky hill

Crossing the Allt Arnan

Despite its modest 684m height, Beinn Damhain's secluded position allows it to stand proud among the higher hills that surround it. It's a shapely hill when viewed from the A82 in upper Glen Falloch and an excellent viewpoint.

Park by the locked gate opposite Glenfalloch farm, (NN 319 196). Space is tight so park carefully to ensure you do not restrict access, and follow the track uphill and over the railway. Go left at the track junction near the pylons and follow the track round into the Làirig Arnan.

As you ascend the glen the hill slowly starts to appear up and to your left. Just before the track ends, follow the second turning down left to a small hydro dam and bridge across the dry gorge of the Allt Arnan, and gain the open hillside beyond. A sheep path is now followed up the left-hand side of the obvious burn which descends the broad hillside left of the summit, from its source in Lochan Beinn Damhain.

Cross over the burn just before the lochan, or by stepping stones at the very mouth of the lochan and gain Beinn Damhain's east ridge. Crossing the burn should be possible in all but the very wildest of spates, when a crossing in bare feet may be necessary!

The ridge gives an unexpectedly interesting ascent over successive humps, to a surprisingly rocky summit cone and the summit cairn with fine views south to **Ben Vorlich** [46] and **Ben Vane** [48], west across Glen Fyne to Beinn Bhuidhe and north to **Ben Lui** [57] and its high companions. Beinn Chabhair and the Crianlarich hills dominate the view to the east. The best return is by the route of ascent.

START & FINISH: *Limited parking near Glenfalloch farm on A82*

DISTANCE: *14.5km; 9 miles;*

TIME: *4hrs 30mins*

MAP: *OS 56; Harvey LLTOA*

TERRAIN: *Tracks and pathless hillside; rough and boggy in places*

GRADE: *Strenuous*

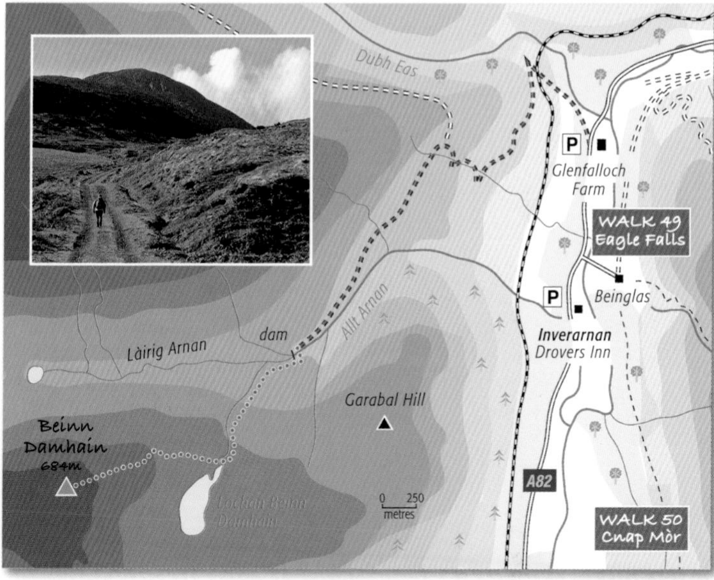

The burn draining Lochan Beinn Damhain below the east ridge

Crianlarich & Tyndrum

Beinn Odhar from Tyndrum

North of Inverarnan and Beinglas, Glen Falloch opens out to the high hills surrounding Crianlarich and Tyndrum. Ben More and Stob Binnein (described in *Loch Lomond and The Trossachs National Park – Vol 2 East*) dominate the view south down Strath Fillan from Tyndrum, although impressive **Cruach Ardrain** [52] takes centre stage closer to Crianlarich.

The north side of Strath Fillan is defined by **Ben Challum** [54], which keeps the charms of its rocky summit ridge well hidden from the glen. The same cannot be said for majestic **Ben Lui** [57] on the south side. At 1130m, this prominent and popular peak is the highest in this book and third highest in the National Park after Ben More, and Stob Binnein.

The next three walks utilise sections of the West Highland Way and explore the political and natural history of the area. **Strath Fillan** [53] follows the River Fillan and **St Fillan's** [55] visits the ruins of the saint's small priory and then explores the glen's agricultural heritage. King Robert I, 'The Bruce', is said to have hurled his armour into the **Lochan of the Lost Sword** [58] following defeat in 1306. Another iconic emblem, the Scots Pine, can be explored in the ancient woodland of the **Beinn Dubhchraig Forest** [56].

Lead mining sustained Tyndrum before the tourists arrived and can be seen at **Tyndrum's Lead Mines** [59] west of the village and on **Beinn Odhar** [60] to the north.

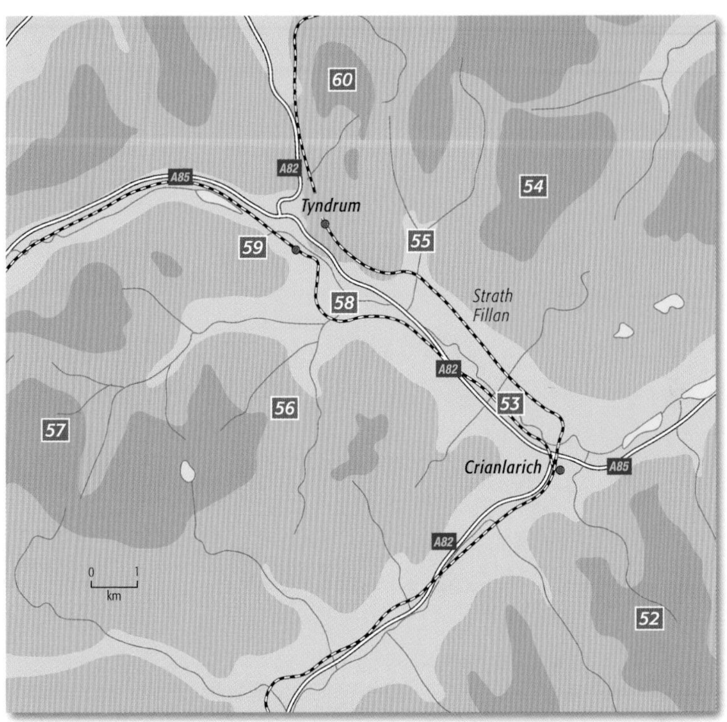

GETTING THERE

Road: *From Glasgow M8, A82. From Edinburgh – M9, A84, A85, A82. From Stirling – A84, A85, A82*

Train: *Scotrail from Glasgow Central (08457 484950), <www.firstgroup.com>*

Bus: *See pages 10 & 11*

TOWNS & VILLAGES

Crianlarich: *Shop, hotels, restaurant, cafe, public toilets*

Tyndrum: *Shops, hotels, restaurants, cafes, public toilets, petrol station*

TOURIST INFORMATION CENTRES (TIC)

Tyndrum: *Main Street (08707 200 626)*

ACCOMMODATION

Widespread hotels and bed and breakfast at Tyndrum and, to a lesser extent, Crianlarich. Scattered bed and breakfast along Strath Fillan. Campsites at Crianlarich (Luib – Glen Dochart), Auchtertyre and Tyndrum. SYHA Youth Hostel at Crianlarich. See also pages 10 & 11

52 Cruach Ardrain

Interesting climbing to a precipitous summit

Cruach Ardrain, centre, from Strath Fillan

Cruach Ardrain is one of the classic high peaks of the National Park, offering a consistantly interesting walk to one of the most precipitous summits in the Southern Highlands. The northern corrie dominates the skyline directly above Crianlarich and was the traditional approach to the mountain for decades. But more recent forestry plantations and logging have complicated this appraoch and the most aesthetic ascent now gains the north-west ridge from Glan Falloch to the west and follows that to the summit

Parking is possible on a section of old road on the south side of the A82 near the end of the long straight before Crianlarich and almost directly below the mountain, (NN 368 238). From the layby cross over the stile and turn immediately left to avoid the worst of the boggy ground, heading for a small mound. Skirt this on the right, to gain a path leading to the track under the railway bridge.

Follow the track up the glen to the

Ben More and Stob Binnein from the summit

START & FINISH: *Layby on the A82 at the head of Glen Falloch*

DISTANCE: *13km; 8 miles*

TIME: *4hrs 30mins*

MAP: *OS 50, 51; Harvey LLTOA*

TERRAIN: *Tracks and paths; boggy and rocky in places*

GRADE: *Strenuous*

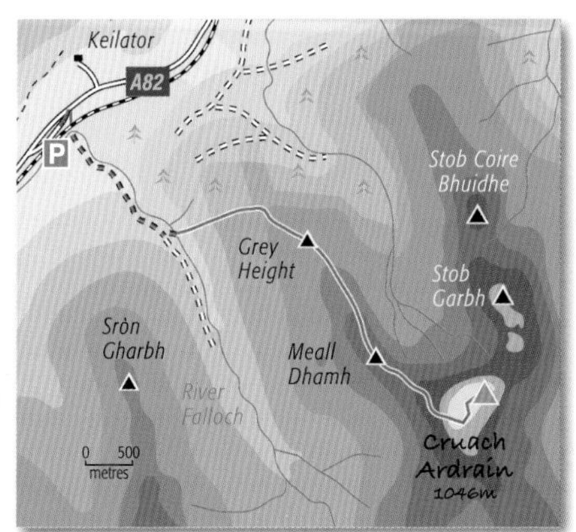

end of the forest and head down left to a small bridge over the River Falloch, below Grey Height. Ascend steeply to gain the ridge and continue ascending to the top of Grey Height. The view north up Strath Fillan is particularly fine with **Ben Challum** [54] prominent on the right above Crianlarich and **Ben Lui** [57] sticking its head above Glen Falloch further to the left.

To the south the north-west ridge leads to the broad bump of Meall Dhamh and round to craggier Cruach Ardrain beyond, with Stob Garbh to its left. It is worth keeping an eye on this latter hill for as height is gained the prominent profiles of Ben More and Stob Binnein start to rise into the sky beside it.

A short scramble over Meall Dhamh gains the base of the summit cone from where a boggy path traverses the west face to gain the south ridge, short of the summit. Turn left and gain the first top and on to the higher exposed summit with a large cairn and a fine view across to Ben More and Stob Binnein. The ascent of both those peaks is described in *Loch Lomond and The Trossachs National Park – Vol 2 East.* Return by the outward route.

West to Ben Lui

53 Strath Fillan

Alongside the River Fillan

South to Ben More and Stob Binnein, left, and Cruach Ardrain, right

Anyone travelling through Strath Fillan sees little of interest from the road. The views to the high hills are excellent, but the glen itself is largely obscured by trees, and any brief clearings reveal only the railway line beside the road.

This circular walk links the West Highland Way on the south side of the glen with fishermen's paths along the banks of the River Fillan on the north side and proves Strath Fillan has much to offer the walker. The river and its banks are wide, but walkers should make a special effort not to disturb fishermen in their quiet recreation.

Start from the small car park on the north side of the A85 in Crianlarich, immediately east of the Glenbruar Viaduct and beside the fire station, (NN 385 254). Cross the road and turn left then right, following signs to the youth hostel and station. Where the road divides keep right for the station and go through the underpass below the tracks and up steps to the main road.

Cross straight over to gain a path ascending through forest to join the main West Highland Way (WHW) path. Turn right onto the waymarked WHW and follow it north for the next 4km (2.5 miles), ignoring turnings to the right and left. The path ascends and descends with good views south to **Cruach Ardrain** [52] and Ben More, east across Strath Fillan to **Ben Challum** [54] and north to **Beinn Odhar** [60] above Tyndrum.

Beyond the turning to Ewich, follow the WHW down beside the Allt an t-Saoir to a railway viaduct, from where a section of the old road leads left to the A82. Cross straight over and through a field to gain the access road to Kirkton Farm and follow it to the far side of the bridge over the River Fillan. Turn right

START & FINISH: *Crianlarich car park on A85*

DISTANCE: *11km; 6.75 miles*

TIME: *3hrs 30mins*

MAP: *OS 50; Harvey LLTOA*

TERRAIN: *Paths; some way-marking, indistinct and wet in places*

GRADE: *Moderate*

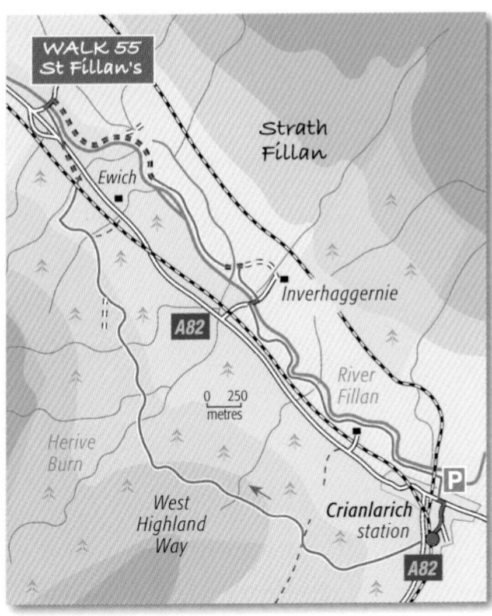

off the WHW onto a track, keep right where it divides, and follow it to where it ends. Cross the fence by the river bank into open broadleaf woodland and follow faint paths close to the raised river bank.

Fishermen's paths between the woodland edge and the river lead round to more open areas of meadow. A few ditches are encountered here and there, but all can be easily crossed or skirted. Follow the riverbank to a large area of gravel, just beyond which a deep tributary makes further progress along the riverbank impossible. However, a track leads inland from the gravel area to a bridge over the tributary, which can then be followed back to the main riverbank path. This leads round to a muddy burn, most easily crossed where it is narrowest, away from the river. The shallower Inverhaggernie Burn is then crossed to gain the access road near Inverhaggernie bridge. If either of these burns prove troublesome to cross then they can be avoided by following the previously mentioned track to the back of Inverhaggernie Farm, crossing through the farmyard and following the access road to the bridge.

Cross over the bridge and turn left following a riverside path to cross a small burn to a gate leading into a field. A well-worn path leads round the field edge beside the river then a tree-lined embankment curving off right, to skirt a boggy area of the riverbank, cut by deep muddy ditches.

Regain the riverbank and follow this round to another very marshy area which is easily skirted on the right via an old metalled track. Beyond this, riverbank paths lead past the house and across the occasional muddy burn to pass below the Glenbruar Viaduct. Turn right and follow the path back to the main road and car park.

North to Beinn Odhar

54 Ben Challum

An extensive mountain with a hidden summit

The summit from the south top

Ben Challum's southern slopes dominate the north side of Strath Fillan, hiding the summit from view and giving the mountain a rather broad and featureless appearance from below. It is only when viewed from a distance that the rocky summit sticks its head above the surrounding landscape. But even then Ben Challum's full character isn't revealed. What appears to be the top actually obscures the higher summit further back. So, in the end the only way to really appreciate Ben Challum is to climb it.

Start from a layby on the south side of the A82 north of Crianlarich, opposite the road leading to the Scottish Agricultural College (SAC) Hill and Mountain Research Centre at Kirkton Farm, (NN 356 280). Cross over and follow the road to join the West Highland Way (WHW) and follow it over the bridge and on towards the farm. Pass the farmhouse on the left to the St Fillan's Priory cemetery and a track crossroads. Continue straight ahead on a rising track – the WHW goes off left – past a second cemetery to reach a level crossing on the railway. This is signposted 'private for authorised users only', so head off right between the wall and the fence for 100 metres, to a footbridge over the railway.

A path starts almost immediately after the footbridge, heading straight up to gain a fenceline which it follows to a deer gate and stile. Pass through an area planted with native trees to exit at a ladder stile and continue to another fence and stile. As the hillside is ascended the view opens out west to Beinn Dubhchraig and **Ben Lui** [57] and south to Ben More, Stob Binnein

START & FINISH: *Layby on the A82 opposite Kirkton*

DISTANCE: *12.5km; 7.75 miles*

TIME: *4hrs 30mins*

MAP: *OS 50; Harvey LLTOA*

TERRAIN: *Tracks and paths; boggy and rocky in places*

GRADE: *Strenuous*

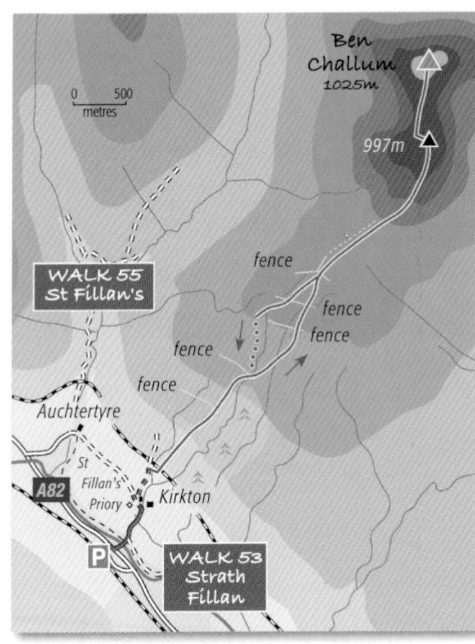

and on to another fence and gate, then climb up onto a broad ridge to a three fence junction and two stiles one ahead and one on the right. Cross over right and follow the obvious path which starts to swing away right from the fenceline, which soon deteriorates into posts only.

A steady rocky slope now leads to the south top with views north to the summit ridge and summit. From the south top drop down to the left to gain the main ridgeline and another path which leads to the main summit marked by a large cairn overlooking the head of Glen Lochay. The return route can be varied at the meeting of the three fences by sticking to the high ground on the right. Follow the path on the broad ridge to before the last rocky knoll which can be avoided on the left by dropping back down to meet the fence before the ladder stile.

and **Cruach Ardrain** [52]. Ahead, Ben Challum's south top and summit start to appear.

Skirt a section of muddy peat hags

Looking west to Ben Lui, left, from above Kirkton farm and the ruins of St Fillan's Priory

55 St Fillan's

Ancient shielings and a ruined priory

Kirkton Farm, Strath Fillan

Strath Fillan gets its name from the now-ruined Saint Fillan's Priory, founded to continue the work of the Irish missionary Fillan. Passing close by the ruins, a section of the West Highland Way links the farms of Kirkton and Auchtertyre, which form the Scottish Agricultural College's Hill and Mountain Research Centre. A number of trails have been established in the area and this walk links some of these with the West Highland Way to give a pleasant walk through contrasting scenery.

North of Crianlarich, leave the A82 at the sign for Auchtertyre wigwams and park in the car park below the farm, (NN 352 289). Here, a signboard in indicates the various walking routes in the area. The paths are wet and muddy in places and good footwear is recommended.

Walk up the road towards the farm and the wooden wigwams and turn left onto the track, just before the bridge. Follow the track to a gate under the railway bridge, and continue with fine views south-east to **Ben Lui** [57] and south-west to Ben More and Stob Binnein. Keep on the track past a sign-board – a shorter alternative goes down right to a bridge over the burn to join the route back – and ascend to a gate.

At a track junction beyond the old shielings an information board states there are some 400 of these old farm buildings in the vicinity. Keep right and descend into the gorge to gain an indistinct path leading down to the bridge below the weir supplying a hydroplant. From here a boardwalk follows the line of the pipe transporting water to the small hydroplant near the farm. Above the lower bridge go left and follow an ascending path to more boardwalk and

START & FINISH: *Auchtertyre Farm car park*

DISTANCE: *9km; 5.5 miles*

TIME: *2hrs 30mins*

MAP: *OS 50; Harvey LLTOA*

TERRAIN: *Waymarked tracks and paths; wet in places*

GRADE: *Easy / Moderate*

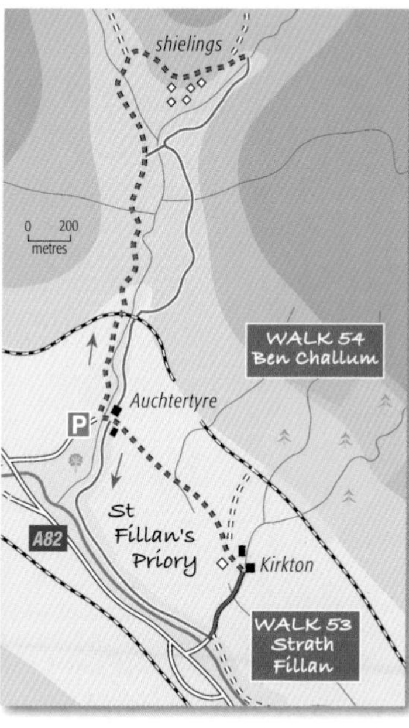

a stile. Further boardwalk and path leads to a fence on the right which can be followed down to the left-hand side of the viaduct where a track is joined. A short way down the track a stile on the right accesses the woodland above the burn and paths leading down to Auchtertyre farm.

Cross straight over the access road and through a small gate. Continue down beside the burn and over a footbridge to gain the riverside, where the path becomes clearer. The going is a little rough so take care not to reach out for the barbed wire fence on your left if you stumble.

This brings you down to the gravel flood plain of the river from where the path goes left between fields and the river to emerge at the access road to Kirkton farm. Turn left onto the West Highland Way and follow it past Kirkton to the ruins of St Fillan's Priory. Keep left following the West Highland Way signs back to Auchtertyre.

Beinn Odhar, left, from the upper glen north of Auchtertyre

56 Dubhchraig Forest

The ancient Scots pines of Coille Coire Chuilc

The ancient Scots pines of Coille Coire Chuilc. Beinn Odhar, right, and Beinn Dorain beyond

Remnants of Scotland's ancient Caledonian Forest are few and far between in the Southern Highlands. Much was felled for timber and agriculture centuries ago, but a few scattered Scots pines cling to the hillsides, their slow growing seedlings protected from grazing deer and sheep by fencing and the lie of the land.

One such area lies at Coille Coire Chuilc on the lower north-eastern flanks of Beinn Dubhchraig, where the River Cononish meets the Allt Gleann Auchreoch. Isolated by the two rivers and surrounded by fencing and larger modern conifer plantations, these Scots pines lead a precarious existence. Ordnance Survey maps from the 1920s show a significantly larger area covered by the trees. While old and aging trees abound, seedlings are thin on the ground. But with a life span of 250 to 300 years, there is still time for regeneration.

From the car park at Dalrigh on the A82, (NN 343 291), gain the old road to the south and follow it left through a gate and past a junction with the West Highland Way, to a bridge over the River Fillan. Turn right onto a track just after the bridge and follow this beside the railway with views straight ahead to Beinn Dubhchraig. Hidden among the glacial moraine debris on the right is Lochan nan Arm, see p154. Pass over the railway and the remnants of Coille Coire Chuilc's Scots pines come into view above the Allt Gleann Auchreoch.

As height is gained on the track, the pines form a fine backdrop to views

START & FINISH: *Dalrigh car park on A82*
DISTANCE: *11km; 6.75 miles*
TIME: *3hrs 45mins*
MAP: *OS 50; Harvey LLTOA*
TERRAIN: *Tracks and paths; very muddy in places*
GRADE: *Moderate*

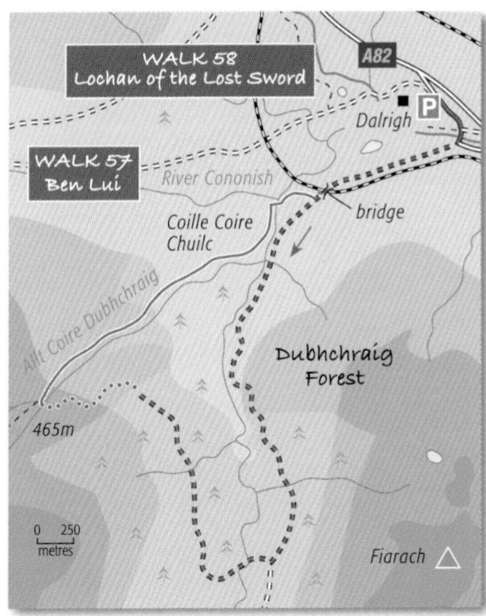

west to Beinn Churin beside Ben Lui and north to the finely shaped peaks of Beinn an Dòthaidh and **Beinn Odhar** [60]. To the east, scattered pines are silhouetted against the bulk of **Ben Challum** [54].

Go through a red gate into the conifer plantation below Beinn Dubhchraig and continue to a track junction. Turn sharply down right to cross the Allt Gleann Auchreoch, then ascend to contour the north-east side of Beinn Dubhchraig to a final zigzag, beyond which the track ends. A faint footpath leads from here towards the Allt Coire Dubhchraig, which is crossed to gain the clear footpath on its north bank. This is the principal route of ascent from Dalrigh to the summit of Beinn Dubhchraig.

Turn right and descend the footpath to a ladder stile into the start of the ancient woodland of birch and Scots pine, and on to another deer fence with assorted holes in it and a broken ladder stile. Pass through as best you can and continue descending, on a path which moves steadily away from the Allt Coire Dubhchraig to arrive at a small bridge over the Allt Gleann Auchreoch, close to its junction with the River Cononish. Cross over and head rightwards to gain the track, the path straight ahead being very muddy.

It should be noted that the path through the forest is well used and can become very muddy in places. Although most of the worst areas can be avoided, adequate footwear is essential.

57 Ben Lui

A classic high peak with a long approach

Ben Lui above the River Cononish

Ben Lui more than holds its own among the outstanding hills of the National Park. Viewed from the south, the peak appears to rise to a single summit of surprising sharpness. Viewed from the east, however, the deeply scoured Coire Gaothach is seen to be enclosed by two steep rocky ridges, each leading to a separate summit and linked by a ridge.

It is the third highest peak in the National Park and the highest in this book (the higher Ben More and Stob Binnein being in Vol 2 – East of this series) and offers a fine expedition. This eastern approach utilises a long track from Tyndrum or Dalrigh and while the going can be hard underfoot, it puts the peak well within the reach of most hillwalkers.

From the car park at Dalrigh on the A82, (NN 343 291), follow the access road back towards the main road and turn left past the houses to gain a track, the route of the West Highland Way. Follow this rightwards across the bridge and past where the West Highland Way goes off to the right.

Pass under the railway line and continue with increasingly open views to Beinn Chuirn and Ben Lui beyond, above the green barns of Cononish farm. Just before a sign on the left highlighting Ben Lui National Nature Reserve, a track joins on the right from Glen Lochy South Forest. This track can also be used to start an ascent of Ben Lui from Tyndrum and is followed by the walk to **Lochan of the Lost Sword** [58]

The track is followed beyond Cononish farm to where it ends at the Allt an Rund burn below Coire Gaothach. Cross over and follow the obvious path up the hillside right of

START & FINISH: *Dalrigh car park on A82, or Tyndrum*

DISTANCE: *18.5km; 11.5 miles*

TIME: *5hrs 30mins*

MAP: *OS 50; Harvey LLTOA*

TERRAIN: *Tracks and paths; rocky in places*

GRADE: *Strenuous*

the burn, passing various cascades to gain the corrie, with the summit looming above.

Once in the corrie the path becomes less distinct and care is needed to keep on route. Stay right of the burn and keep an eye out for the continuation path which ascends steadily north-west below Stob Garbh, the high point on the right-hand ridge of the corrie, to gain the col between Coire Gaothach and Coire an Lochain to the north.

From the col follow the steeper and rockier north ridge with fine positions on the lip of the steep headwall of Coire Gaothach, to gain the lower north top. From there a short ridge leads to the summit cairn. As would be expected the views are extensive from Ben Nevis and Glen Coe to Mull, Arrochar and Arran. Return by the route of ascent.

Ben Lui from the east

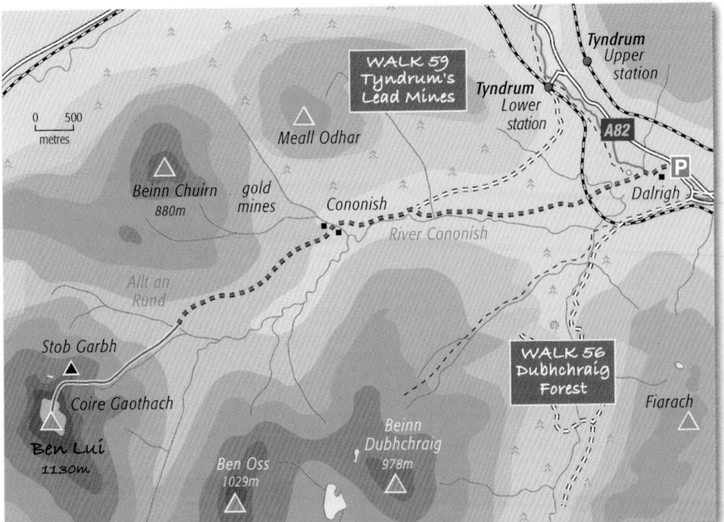

The summit of Ben Lui from the North Top

58 Lochan of the Lost Sword

The escape of King Robert I, 'The Bruce'

Ben More and Stob Binnein from Lochan of the Lost Sword

Strath Fillan is littered with moraine debris and glacial lochans, features which have changed little since the glaciers covering the Highlands began to melt, some 10,000 years ago.

According to legend one of these deep lochans also contains the broadsword and battle armour of the King of Scotland. Here, Robert I, 'The Bruce', and his men are said to have cast off their heavy weaponry and made good their escape, following defeat at the battle of Dalrigh in 1306.

Bruce fled south via Loch Lomond – Stùic an t-Iobairt or Bruce's Tree lies south of Tarbet on the loch's west shore – before crossing to Rathlin Island off Ireland. The following year he returned to Scotland to continue his fight for an independent Scotland, which culminated at Bannockburn in 1314.

Exactly which lochan received all this ironwork is not clear. The lochan to the north visited by this walk is credited as the spot and has a commemoration stone carved with a broadsword. However, the lochan to the south is named Lochan nan Arm (Lochan of the Weapon) on the Ordnance Survey 1:25,000 map. We will probably never know which lochan it was, or even if the story is true.

The walk is described starting from the car park off the A82 at Dalrigh, (NN 343 291), but could as easily be started from Tyndrum. From the car park follow the access road back towards the main road and turn left past the houses to gain a track, the route of the West

START & FINISH: *Dalrigh car park on A82, or Tyndrum*

DISTANCE: *8km; 5 miles*

TIME: *2hrs 30mins*

MAP: *OS 50; Harvey LLTOA*

TERRAIN: *Tracks and paths; some waymarking*

GRADE: *Easy*

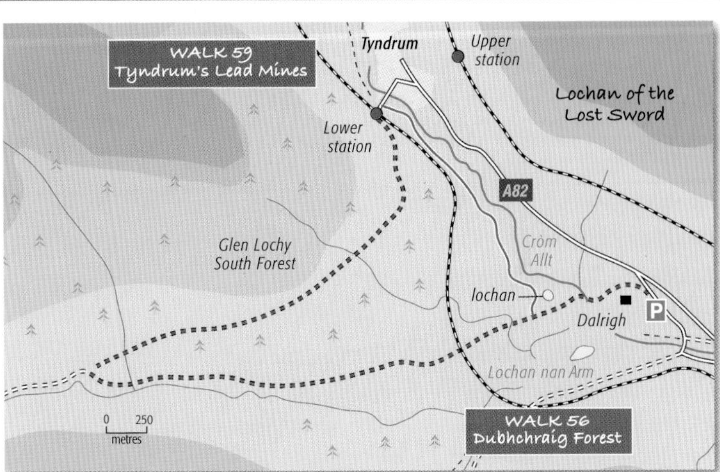

Highland Way. Follow this rightwards across the bridge and ascend to where the Way leaves the track for a path on the right. The track continues to Cononish farm and **Ben Lui** [57], and is the return route for this walk.

Tyndrum Lower station and Ben More

Follow the path right to arrive quite quickly at the so-called Lochan of the Lost Sword, with its fine backdrop of Ben More, Stob Binnein and **Cruach Ardrain** [52]. Continue on the West Highland Way towards Tyndrum passing through a barren area where lead ore was once sluiced. As the information board points out, the toxicity of the ore means that sections of land such as this support few plants to this day.

A fine section of woodland alongside the Cròm Allt leads to a road on the outskirts of Tyndrum. Turn left to the car park of Tyndrum Lower station, cross over the railway at the gates and turn left onto a track through the conifer plantation. This section of the walk is a pleasant change of direction and the track contours the hillside gradually to drop down to the Cononish farm track. The head of the glen is filled with the high hills of Ben Lui, Ben Oss and Beinn Dubhchraig. Turn left and follow the track back to Dalrigh.

59 Tyndrum's Lead Mines

Industrial archaeology in the Highlands

Tyndrum and Ben Challum from the mines

Tyndrum has a long history of lead mining and the scars are clear on the hillside above the village. This and the following walk visit some of the old mines where galena was extracted, washed, crushed and taken to Loch Lomond for smelting. It was then floated down the loch and the River Leven and up the Clyde for the roofs and water pipes of Glasgow. Fences cordon off the old shafts visible on this walk and all are deep, internally unstable and surrounded by loose rock.

Park at either the Tourist Information Centre, or the minimarket, on the right, just after the bridge at the north end of the village. Opposite the minimarket, follow the West Highland Way south past a row of old cottages to where the access road ends and a path begins.

At the path junction turn right onto a path with an Acorn waymark – the mine workings are clear on the hillside up ahead – and follow the path beside the river and down left to pass under the railway via a 'cattle creep' bridge. This can be wet and slippery, as a burn also flows under the bridge.

Follow the burn to where the Acorn path curves round left to gain a forest firebreak leading back to Tyndrum.

START & FINISH: *Tyndrum car parks on A82*

DISTANCE: *6.5km; 4 miles*

TIME: *2hrs 30mins*

MAP: *OS 50; Harvey LLTOA*

TERRAIN: *Tracks and paths; some waymarking, rocky and wet in places*

GRADE: *Moderate*

Don't follow this, it will be utilised on the return, but turn right across the burn to gain a trackway leading into conifer woodland and an obvious path.

Maintain the easiest line up through the woodland, the path becomes grassier and faint in places, heading steadily right to gain the long tongue of rock waste below the mines. Ascend the scree out of the trees, keeping right of the fence, to where a path starts to move rightwards, then zigzags up the debris-strewn hillside. The wide, rocky path acts as a streambed and can be quite wet in places.

When the hillside becomes more craggy, the path traverses way out right into the heather to join and follow a small burn, before returning back left to the drier mine debris. The high point of the workings is marked by the remains of two stone buildings, with the tops of mine shafts visible beyond the fence.

A return can be made from here, although the small summit of Sròn nan Colan lies just above and can be ascended by continuing on the zigzag path to join and follow a fence. At the crest, an old fenceline leads right over two rocky knolls to the cairned summit.

Tyndrum lead mines

Return by descending the zigzags and the scree into the forest. The scree becomes grassy then bare again and shortly after this, veer right onto the ascent path and follow it straight down past old sluice pens and debris to arrive back at the burn above the bridge. Turn right and follow the waymarked track along the forest firebreak with views to Ben More and Stob Binnein, to arrive at the railway. Cross over and through the car park, then left through a gate onto the West Highland Way, which leads over a ford back to the start.

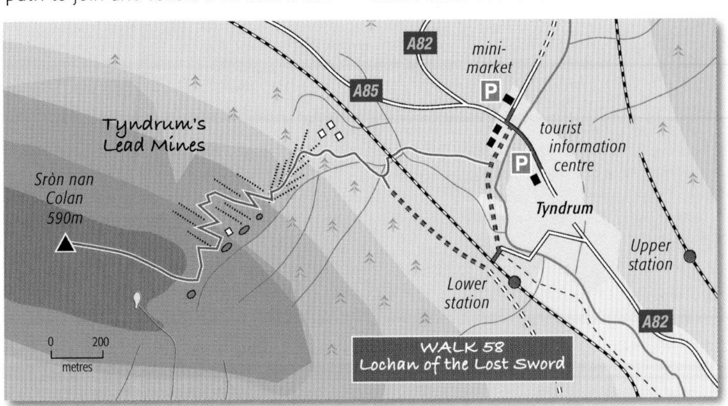

60 Beinn Odhar

A fine peak with even finer views

Beinn Odhar, right, and Beinn Dorain from the West Highland Way

Beinn Odhar presents an impressive profile when viewed from Tyndrum village. It is a lot less steep than it looks and offers a steady ascent, with a couple of old lead mines en route for added interest. The hill is easily accessed from either the car park by the Tourist Information Centre, or from the car park by the minimarket, on the right just after the bridge at the north end of the village. Follow the West Highland Way northwards from the minimarket to where it crosses the railway and the Cròm Allt, which flows from the hill's southern corrie.

Go through the gate and take to the hillside, heading rightwards to a grassy track following the raised left bank of the Cròm Allt. After a short distance the track fades and appears to divide and you leave the burn to ascend a ridge on the hillside, aiming for the prominent crags high above you.

Zigzag up the hillside, following occasional sections of old grassy track, to arrive at tongues of rock debris from the mining. Two mines can be found on the far side of the crags where a vein of the lead bearing mineral galena runs vertically up the hillside. The mines are old and dangerous and should not be entered.

The hillside now levels out at a lochan from where final boulderly slopes gain the summit ridge. The views west from the summit to Beinn Dubhchraig and **Ben Lui [57]** are particularly fine, but it is the view north to Beinn Dorain, with Ben Nevis in the